CONDOLEEZZA
RICE

*a memoir of my
extraordinary, ordinary
family and me*

CONDOLEEZZA
RICE

a memoir of my
extraordinary, ordinary
family and me

condoleezza rice

EMBER

All rights reserved. Published in the United States by Ember, an imprint of Random House Children's Books,
a division of Random House, Inc., New York. Originally published in hardcover in the United States by Delacorte
Press, an imprint of Random House Children's Books, New York, in 2010. This work is based upon *Extraordinary,
Ordinary People: A Memoir by Condoleezza Rice*, copyright © 2010 by Condoleezza Rice, published in hardcover by
Crown Publishers, an imprint of the Crown Publishing Group, a division of Random House, Inc., New York, in 2010.

Ember and the colophon are trademarks of Random House, Inc.

Grateful acknowledgment is made to the following for permission to reprint previously published material:

Alfred Publishing Co., Inc.: Lyrics from "Take My Hand, Precious Lord," words and music by
Thomas A. Dorsey, copyright © 1938 (Renewed) by Warner-Tamerlane Publishing Corp.
All rights reserved. Reprinted by permission of Alfred Publishing Co., Inc.

Hal Leonard Corporation: Lyrics from "Theme from 'The Greatest American Hero,'" from the television series, words
by Stephen Geyer, music by Mike Post, copyright © 1981 by EMI Blackwood Music Inc., Dar-Jen Music, EMI April
Music Inc. and Stephen Cannell Music. All rights for Dar-Jen Music controlled and administered by EMI Blackwood
Music Inc. All rights reserved. International copyright secured. Reprinted by permission of Hal Leonard Corporation.

Visit us on the Web! randomhouse.com/kids
and randomhouse.com/teens

Educators and librarians, for a variety of teaching tools, visit us at randomhouse.com/teachers

The Library of Congress has cataloged the hardcover edition of this work as follows:
Rice, Condoleezza.
Condoleezza Rice : a memoir of my extraordinary, ordinary family and me / Condoleezza Rice. — 1st ed.
p. cm. ISBN 978-0-385-73879-8 (hardcover trade) — ISBN 978-0-385-90747-7 (glb) — ISBN 978-0-375-89613-
2 (ebook) [1. Rice, Condoleezza, 1954– —Juvenile literature. 2. Rice, Condoleezza, 1954– —Family—Juvenile
literature. 3. Women cabinet officers—United States—Biography—Juvenile literature. 4. Cabinet officers—United
States—Biography—Juvenile literature. 5. African American women educators—Biography—Juvenile literature. 6.
African American women—Biography—Juvenile literature. 7. Alabama—Biography—Juvenile literature.] I. Title.
E840.8.R48.A3 2010b
327.730092—dc22
2010029878

ISBN 978-0-385-73880-4 (tr. pbk.)

RL: 5.9

Printed in the United States of America

10 9 8 7 6 5 4 3 2 1

First Ember Edition 2012

Random House Children's Books supports the First Amendment and celebrates the right to read.

To my parents,
John and Angelena Rice,
and my grandparents:
Mattie and Albert Ray,
and John and Theresa Rice

contents

author's note

My parents, John and Angelena Rice, were extraordinary, ordinary people. They were middle-class folks who loved God, family, and their country. They loved each other unreservedly and built a world together that wove the fibers of our life—faith, family, community, and education—into a seamless tapestry of high expectations and unconditional love. I don't think they ever read a book on parenting. They were just good at it—not perfect, but really good. Somehow they raised their little girl in Jim Crow Birmingham, Alabama, to believe that even if she couldn't have a hamburger at the Woolworth's lunch counter, she could be president of the United States.

As it became known that I was writing a book about my parents, I received many letters and emails from people who knew my mom and dad, telling me how my parents had touched their lives. In conducting this journey into the past I also had the pleasure of returning to the places my parents lived and talking with their friends, associates, and students. I am so glad I had the chance to connect with so many who knew them.

I was also contacted by people who *didn't* know my parents but recognized in my story their own parents' love and sacrifice. Good parents are a blessing. Mine were determined to give me a chance to live a unique and happy life. In that they succeeded, and that is why every night I begin my prayers saying, "Lord, I can never thank you enough for the parents you gave me."

CONDOLEEZZA
RICE

*a memoir of my
extraordinary, ordinary
family and me*

chapter one

By all accounts, my parents approached the time of my birth with great anticipation. My father was certain that I'd be a boy and had worked out a deal with my mother: if the baby was a girl, *she* would name her, but a boy would be named John.

Mother started thinking about names for her daughter. She wanted a name that would be unique and musical. Looking to Italian musical terms for inspiration, she at first settled on Andantino. But realizing that it translated as "moving slowly," she decided that she didn't like the implications of that name. Allegro was worse because it translated as "fast," and no mother in 1954 wanted her daughter to be thought of as "fast." Finally she found the musical terms *con dolce* and *con dolcezza*, meaning "with sweetness." Deciding that an English speaker would never recognize the hard *c*, saying "dolci" instead of "dolche," my mother doctored the term. She settled on Condoleezza.

Meanwhile, my father prepared for John's birth. He bought a football and several other pieces of sports equipment. John was going to be an all-American running back or perhaps a linebacker.

My mother thought she felt labor pains on Friday night, November 12, and was rushed to the doctor. Dr. Plump, the black pediatrician who delivered most of the black babies in town, explained that it was probably just anxiety. He decided nonetheless to put Mother in the hospital, where she could rest comfortably.

The public hospitals were completely segregated in Birmingham, with the Negro wards—no private rooms were available—in the basement. There wasn't much effort to separate maternity cases from patients with any other kind of illness, and by all accounts the accommodations were pretty grim. As a result, mothers who could get in preferred to birth their babies at Holy Family, the Catholic hospital that segregated white and Negro patients but at least had something of a maternity floor and private rooms. Mother checked into Holy Family that night.

Nothing happened on Saturday or early Sunday morning. Dr. Plump told my father to go ahead and deliver his sermon at the eleven o'clock church service. "This baby isn't going to be born for quite a while," he said.

He was wrong. When my father came out of the pulpit at noon on November 14, his mother was waiting for him in the church office.

"Johnny, it's a girl!"

Daddy was floored. "A girl?" he asked. "How could it be a girl?"

He rushed to the hospital to see the new baby. Daddy told me that the first time he saw me in the nursery, the other babies were just lying still, but I was trying to raise myself up. Now, I think it's doubtful that an hours-old baby was strong enough to do this. But my father insisted this story was true. In any case, he said that his heart melted at the sight of his baby girl. From that day on he was a "feminist"—there was nothing that his little girl couldn't do, including learning to love football.

chapter two

My parents were anxious to give me a head start in life—perhaps a little too anxious. My first memory of confronting them and in a way declaring my independence was a conversation concerning their ill-conceived attempt to send me to first grade at the ripe age of three. My mother was teaching at Fairfield Industrial High School in Fairfield, Alabama, and the idea was to enroll me in the elementary school located on the same campus. I don't know how they talked the principal into going along, but sure enough, on the first day of school in September 1958, my mother took me by the hand and walked me into Mrs. Jones's classroom.

I was terrified of the other children and of Mrs. Jones, and I refused to stay. Each day we would repeat the scene, and each day my father would have to pick me up and take me to my grandmother's house, where I would stay until the school day ended. Finally I told my mother that I didn't want to go back because the teacher wore the same skirt every morning. I am sure this was not literally true. Perhaps I somehow already understood that my mother believed in good grooming and appropriate attire. Anyway, Mother and Daddy got the point and abandoned their attempt at *really* early childhood education.

I now think back on that time and laugh. John and Angelena were prepared to try just about anything—or to let me try just about anything—that could be called an educational opportunity. They were convinced that education was a kind of armor shielding me against everything—even the deep racism in Birmingham and across America.

They were bred to those views. They were both born in the South at the height of segregation and racial prejudice—Mother just outside of Birmingham, Alabama, in 1924 and Daddy in Baton Rouge, Louisiana, in 1923. They were of the first generation of middle-class blacks to attend historically black colleges—institutions that previously had been for the children of the black elite. And like so many of their peers, they rigorously controlled their environment to preserve their dignity and their pride.

Objectively, white people had all the power and blacks had none. "The White Man," as my parents called "them," controlled politics and the economy. This depersonalized collective noun spoke to the fact that my parents and their friends had few interactions with whites that were truly personal. In his wonderful book *Colored People*, Harvard Professor Henry Louis "Skip" Gates Jr. recalled that his family and friends in West Virginia addressed white people by their professions—for example, "Mr. Policeman" or "Mr.

Milkman." Black folks in Birmingham didn't even have that much contact. It was just "The White Man."

Certainly, in any confrontation with a white person in Alabama you were bound to lose. But my parents believed that you could alter that equation through education, hard work, perfectly spoken English, and an appreciation for the "finer things" in "their" culture. If you were twice as good as they were, "they" might not like you but "they" had to respect you. You could find space for a fulfilling and productive life. There was nothing worse than being a helpless victim of your circumstances. My parents were determined to avoid that. Needless to say, they were even more determined that I not end up that way.

chapter three

My parents were not blue bloods. Yes, there were blue bloods who were black. These were the prominent black families that had emerged after the Civil War, though many of their patriarchs had been freed well before slavery ended. These families had produced black lawyers and doctors in the late nineteenth century; some of them even included political figures, such as Hiram Rhodes Revels, the first black United States senator. There were pockets of these families in the Northeast and a large colony in Chicago. Some had even attended Ivy League schools, but others, particularly those from the South, sent their children to such respected institutions as Meharry Medical College, Fisk, Morehouse, Spelman, and the Tuskegee Institute. In some cases these families had been college-educated for several generations.

My mother's family was not from this caste, though it was more patrician than my father's. Mattie Lula Parrom, my maternal grandmother, was the daughter of a high-ranking official, perhaps a bishop, in the African Methodist Episcopal Church. Though details about her father, my great-grandfather, are sketchy, he was able to provide my grandmother with a first-rate education for a "colored" girl of that time. Grandmother had rich brown skin and very high cheekbones, exposing American Indian blood that was obvious, if ill-defined. She was deeply religious, unfailingly trusting in God, and cultured.

My grandfather Albert Robinson Ray III was one of six siblings, extremely fair-skinned and possibly the product of a white father and a black mother. There was also apparently an Italian branch of the family on his mother's side, memorialized in the names of successive generations. There are several Altos; my mother and her grandmother were named Angelena; my aunt was named Genoa (though, as Southerners, we pronounce her name "Gen-OH-a"); my cousin is Lativia; and I am Condoleezza, all attesting to that part of our heritage.

Granddaddy Ray's story is a bit hazy because he ran away from home when he was thirteen and did not reconnect with his family until he was an adult. According to family lore, Granddaddy used a tire iron to beat a white man who had assaulted his sister. Fearing for his life, he ran away and later found himself sitting in a train station in the wee hours of the morning, a single token in his pocket. As Granddaddy sat alone in that station, a white man came over and asked what he was doing there at that hour. For reasons that are not entirely clear, "Old Man Wheeler," as he was known in our family, took my grandfather home and raised him with his sons.

I remember going to my grandmother's house in 1965 to tell her that Granddaddy had passed away at the hospital. She wailed and soon said, "Somebody call the Wheeler boys." One came over to the house immediately. They were obviously just like family.

I've always been struck by this story because it speaks to the complicated history of blacks and whites in America. We came to this country as founding populations—Europeans and Africans. Our bloodlines have crossed and been intertwined by the ugly sexual exploitation that was very much a part of slavery. Even in the depths of segregation, blacks and whites lived very close to each other. There are the familiar stories of black nannies who were "a part of the family," raising the wealthy white children for whom they cared. But there are also inexplicable stories like that of my grandfather and the Wheelers.

We still have a lot of trouble with the truth of how tangled our family histories are. These legacies are painful and remind us of America's birth defect: slavery. I can remember being asked how I felt when I learned that I apparently had two white great-grandfathers, one on each side of the family. I just considered it a fact—no feelings were necessary. We all have white ancestors, and some whites have black ancestors.

It is just easier not to talk about all of this or to obscure it with the term "African American," which recalls the immigration narrative. There are groups such as Mexican Americans, Korean Americans, and German Americans who retain a direct link to their immigrant ancestors. But the fact is that only a portion of those with black skin are direct descendants of African immigrants. One of these is President

Obama, who was born of a white American mother and a Kenyan father. Then there is a second narrative that involves immigrants from the West Indies, such as Colin Powell's parents. And what of the descendants of slaves in the old Confederacy? I prefer "black" and "white." These terms are starker and remind us that the first Europeans and the first Africans came to this country together—the Africans in chains.

chapter four

One day Granddaddy Ray passed a beautiful young girl drawing water at a well. He introduced himself, but when he
learned that she was only sixteen, he refrained from trying to
date her. When she was finally old enough, Mattie Lula Parrom and Albert Ray married. Albert was industrious and
worked three jobs for most of his life. He labored as an engi-
neer in the coal mines during the week, a profession that sad-
dled him with emphysema and heart disease and gave him a
deep admiration for John L. Lewis and the coal miners'
union; he sheared horses in the evening, a skill that he'd
been taught by Mr. Wheeler; and on the weekends he built
houses. Granddaddy's day began every morning at four
o'clock with Grandmother cooking a big breakfast of steak or
bacon and eggs to sustain him through the hard workday
ahead.

The Rays were proud people. They settled in Hooper

City, Alabama, which in those days was pretty far outside the city limits of Birmingham. Even when I was a child my grandparents' home felt as though it were in the country, not the city.

Mattie and Albert Ray were landowners who built their house with their own hands. The white wood-framed home was large for its time, on a corner lot with a big pecan tree in the front yard. It had eight large rooms, including a music room where my grandmother taught piano. Grandmother loved fine things, and the heavy mahogany furniture, always purchased with cash, survives in various family members' houses—including my own—to this very day.

My aunts and uncle remember their parents' determination to maintain their dignity despite the degrading circumstances of Birmingham. The children were constantly reminded, "You are a Ray!" This was both an admonition to let nothing hold them back and occasionally a rebuke when my grandparents disapproved of their behavior. They were never allowed to use a "colored" restroom or water fountain. "Wait until you get home," they were told. And my grandparents always made sure that they had a car so that no one had to ride in the back of the bus.

My mother had five siblings. Albert junior, Mattie, and my mother were born very close together in the early 1920s. Uncle Alto and Aunt Genoa, who went by Gee, made their entrance about a decade later. My grandparents were not themselves college-educated, but they were determined that their children would be. As it turned out, this took some doing, but all five eventually finished college.

Both my mother and her older sister, Mattie, went to

Miles College in Fairfield, Alabama. They lived at home and drove to college each day. Both were stunningly beautiful. Mattie looked like her mother, sharing her rich brown complexion, high cheekbones, and long, wavy black hair. My mother looked like her father, fair-skinned with the same round face that I have, and she had long, straight brownish hair. As little girls they were favored by adults because they were so cute. One of my most cherished photographs shows five-year-old Mattie and three-year-old Angelena posing for the local barbershop's calendar.

In college the Ray girls were popular, with outgoing Mattie becoming a majorette and my more reserved mother breaking out of character by becoming a cheerleader. Mattie, who played high school and collegiate tennis and basketball, was a real athlete. My mother, however, was not. In order to fulfill her physical education requirement, she created a scrapbook. Her teacher gave her a B for the beautiful work but told her he just couldn't give her an A when she didn't even break a sweat. She was an artist and a lady, and she didn't really believe that women should play sports or, heaven forbid, perspire. I can't remember my mother ever picking up a bat or a ball of any kind, and though she later learned to enjoy spectator sports with my father and me, she never fully came to terms with my tomboy tendencies.

After college Mattie and Angelena continued to live at home. My mother and her sister had many friends, but they were clearly each other's best friend. Life in segregated Birmingham was in some ways pretty simple: family, church, work, and a social life built around black fraternities and private clubs. Mother and her sister became well-regarded teachers at the same high school, though their perpetual tardiness led their father to set the house clocks far ahead to force them to be on time. They'd been taught music by their mother and grandmother, and on Sundays they played organ and piano for Baptist churches—they were Methodists themselves, but the Baptists paid better.

On the weekend, the girls went to fraternity and social club dances in dresses that Mattie, who could sew beautifully, made from whatever material they liked. They loved clothes. My mother once said that her meager teacher's salary was already owed to fine clothing stores such as Burger-Phillips and Newberry's the minute she got it. They took trips to shop in downtown Birmingham, where their really light-skinned acquaintances would "pass" as white so that they could go to lunch counters and bring hot dogs out to their waiting, darker-skinned friends, who could not get served.

My mother had been teaching at Fairfield Industrial High for several years when a new athletic director and assistant football coach was hired. Tall, dark-skinned, and extremely athletic, he was powerfully built and had a deep, resonant voice. And he was a preacher who happened to be single. Mother claimed that John Wesley Rice Jr. first saw her walking down the hallway in a red polka-dot dress and red, very high-heeled strappy shoes. He was leaning against the wall, filing his fingernails and hoping to have a chance to say hello. He claimed that it was *she* who had made the first move, dressing that way to catch his attention.

Daddy had come to Birmingham after finishing Johnson C. Smith University in Charlotte, North Carolina. He'd started school at Stillman College in Alabama, but when World War II broke out, Granddaddy decided to send him to Smith, where he could attend college and then go on to seminary. Daddy wanted to go into the army but acceded to his father's wishes. He did do some chaplain's work for soldiers returning from the front, but I think he always felt a little guilty for not having fought in the war.

In any case, by the time Daddy arrived at Fairfield High School, he had already been pastor of his first church and had worked several jobs simultaneously. On the weekends he played and coached semiprofessional football in Burlington, North Carolina. Sometimes he worked as a waiter to supplement his income, and he even tried opening a restaurant, which failed miserably. Until the day he died he always tipped generously, saying that waiting tables was the hardest work he had ever done.

My paternal grandfather, John Wesley Rice Sr., was born in Eutaw (pronounced "UH-tah"), Alabama. Not many blacks owned land in those days, so my grandfather's family worked the land of others as sharecroppers. Granddaddy's father was illiterate, but his mother, my great-grandmother Julia Head, was a freed slave who'd learned to read. It isn't clear who educated her, since it was illegal to teach slaves to read. But she was apparently a favored house slave, and there is a story that Julia ran Union soldiers off the plantation and protected the horses during the Civil War. Perhaps she thought she'd have to do it again, because until the day she died, she would sit on her porch with a shotgun in her lap and a pipe in her mouth.

According to my father, Granddaddy Rice was not a

favored son because, unlike his siblings, he was very dark-skinned. You will notice that I have by now described the skin color of each of my relatives. Unfortunately, it mattered. One of the scars of slavery was a deep preoccupation with skin color in the black community. The lighter your skin, the better off you were. This bias extended to other facial features: thin and "Caucasian" was preferred to thick and "Negroid," just as straight hair was "good" compared to kinky hair, which was "bad." The repercussions were significant in my parents' time, when no self-respecting black school would select a dark-skinned homecoming queen. There was even rumored to be a "paper bag test" for membership in the best clubs—if you were any darker than a paper bag, you needn't bother to apply.

By the time I came along, skin color and other physical features were less important, though not irrelevant. My father loved that I had my mother's long hair, despite the fact that mine, unlike hers, was a coarse, thick, and somewhat unruly mop. When I finally cut it in college, it was pretty clear that he thought I'd given up some sort of social advantage. But by then the "black is beautiful" aesthetic and Afro hairstyles had introduced a new concept of what was appealing.

One can imagine, though, what it was like for my very dark-skinned grandfather in the first half of the twentieth century. He was given the worst land to work and not much encouragement from his father. But his mother taught him to read and sent him to school. He had big dreams and loved books. So when he was about nineteen he decided to get a college education. He asked people, in the parlance of the day, how a "colored" man could go to college. They told him about little Stillman College, which was about thirty miles away in Tuscaloosa, Alabama. He saved his cotton and paid the school.

After one year, though, Granddaddy Rice ran out of cotton and had no way to pay his tuition. He was told that he would have to leave. Thinking quickly, he pointed to some of his fellow students. "How are those boys going to college?" he asked. He was told that they'd earned a scholarship and that he could have one too if he wanted to be a Presbyterian minister. Without missing a beat, Granddaddy Rice replied, "Well, that's exactly what I had in mind." As they would do several times in my family's history, the Presbyterians educated this young black man.

John Wesley Rice Sr. soon met Theresa Hardnett, a pretty half-Creole from Baton Rouge. The Hardnett family produced educated girls, including two who were among the first black registered nurses to graduate from Booker T. Washington's Tuskegee Institute. My grandmother, though, left home when she was seventeen and married my grandfather shortly thereafter. She set out with him on his mission of church building and educational evangelism.

While my mother's family was landowning and settled, Daddy's family lived the life of an itinerant preacher. As a result, my parents held very different views on the importance of land. Mother always wanted to own a house and sometimes, a little pointedly, reminded Daddy that he'd grown up moving from place to place and living in "other people's houses." Her family, on the other hand, had owned land. Daddy didn't really care and felt a bit tied down by the financial responsibility of home ownership. While they did eventually own property and a house, their differences on this matter remained a source of some conflict throughout their marriage.

In any case, Granddaddy Rice worked mostly in Louisiana, founding a church and a school next door. Sometimes he found it necessary to work in Mississippi and Alabama, leaving the family behind for a few months in Louisiana. Granddaddy's churches were successful because he was a powerful speaker. His sermons were intellectually sound and biblically based. He made it clear that he'd studied theology in seminary and was a fully ordained minister. In his sermons, there was none of the "whooping and hollering" emotion of the Baptists across town, who had no formal training. Granddaddy apparently delivered his sermons without notes. I once told my father that I was grateful that I'd inherited his exceptional ability to speak off the cuff. He told me that he was indeed good but not like Granddaddy. "You should have heard your grandfather," he said. "He spoke in whole paragraphs."

The Rice schools were even more successful than the churches. My grandfather believed that his schools could better educate black children than the miserable public schools of the day, and he sought funds from any source he could, whether it meant a few cents from parents in the community or fifty dollars from rich white people across town. Granddaddy Rice once told Daddy that "white guilt" was his best ally in funding his schools. But when a white church collected a bunch of old textbooks and "donated" them to my grandfather's school, he politely declined. It was important, he explained, that his kids have the most up-to-date reading materials, just like the white students.

Granddaddy's educational evangelism compelled him to go door-to-door in the poor neighborhoods around him and impress upon parents the importance of sending their kids to college. Then he would go to colleges—usually Presbyterian schools such as Stillman, Johnson C. Smith, and Knoxville College in Tennessee—and "make arrangements" for the kids to go there. In turn, he would recruit young teachers from the historically black colleges with which he had these relationships. He was zealously committed to education because he believed that it had transformed him, and he was determined to spread its benefits.

When it came to his own family, he was even more insistent. My father and his sister, Theresa, attended schools their father had founded most recently. When it came time for high school, Granddaddy placed his kids in Baton Rouge's McKinley High, which in 1916 had graduated the first class of black students in the state of Louisiana.

Growing up, my father was a very good athlete but not a great student, as he remembered it. It was a struggle to get him to study, and he didn't love to read, though he loved history and politics. For the most part, Daddy seems to have enjoyed less serious pursuits. He loved to play preacher. One day he and his sister re-created a funeral that their father had just conducted. They went to the church, set their dolls up in the pews, and laid one doll on the altar table to mimic a casket. Theresa was playing the piano, and my father had begun to preach when one of the dolls in the pew fell with a heavy thud. They ran out as fast as possible, sure that they'd somehow awakened the dead.

Daddy was an easygoing personality who didn't always take life too seriously. He was a popular kid who would become an outgoing adult. His sister, Theresa, by contrast, was reclusive, brilliant, and determined to follow in her father's intellectual footsteps. She would later go on to become one of the first black women to receive a doctorate in English literature from the University of Wisconsin. Thus I am not even the first PhD in my family.

Aunt Theresa wrote books on Charles Dickens, including one called *Dickens and the Seven Deadly Sins*. When I was about eight years old, we were visiting Aunt Theresa in Baton Rouge, where she was teaching at Southern University. When I saw that she was reading A *Tale of Two Cities*, I asked whether she'd ever read that book before. "I have read this novel at least twenty-five times," she said. I remember thinking that this was a terribly boring way to spend one's life. For years it soured my thoughts of being a professor, since I associated the vocation with the drudgery of reading the same book twenty-five times.

chapter five

It took my parents a long time to finally tie the knot. They began "courting," as my mother called it, almost immediately after meeting, but they did not marry for almost three years. I soon learned, both from their recollections and from stories told by others in the community, that these young sweethearts were apparently the talk of the town—while teaching their classes, my parents often passed notes to each other through student couriers.

The two young teachers were fully committed to their work. Mother taught English. Her former students remember her as a teacher whom you didn't disobey despite her diminutive stature. She was a stickler for good grammar. She was the coach of the debate team and would enter her students in citywide oratorical contests. She also directed student plays and musicals, gaining a sterling reputation throughout the city for her efforts.

Her most famous student, though, was neither a debater nor a thespian. Mother taught American baseball legend Willie Mays and, despite her lack of sports acumen, knew that he was special. He recently told me that he remembered her well and recalled that she had told him early on, "You're going to be a ballplayer. If you need to leave a little early for practice, you let me know."

During my parents' courtship, Daddy's workday was completely tied up with sports. Daddy had studied athletic administration at the University of Wisconsin and put that knowledge to work by creating a comprehensive sports program. He started a girls' basketball team, which he held to the same rigorous standards of technical excellence that he demanded of the boys.

The young couple also enjoyed an expansive social life outside of school. Birmingham was so segregated that most middle-class social activities took place in private homes and private social clubs. The few public spaces for blacks weren't very desirable and were located in rough neighborhoods such as Fourth Avenue in downtown Birmingham. The area was known for drinking, knife fights, and "loose" women. Though my father seems to have gone to the movie theater in that part of town once in a while, my mother stayed away. In those days, there was a very clear distinction between "nice girls" and "bad girls," and one had to be very careful about one's reputation.

Fortunately, there seem to have been many private functions. Daddy was a member of Alpha Phi Alpha, the oldest black fraternity, which sponsored dances and parties. Thankfully, Daddy was a *Presbyterian* minister, not a Southern

Baptist, and so dancing and even a little light drinking by the minister were quite acceptable to the congregation. To the end of his life, Daddy's eyes would fill with tears when a band played "Stars Fell on Alabama," which was always the last dance of the night.

My parents' lives, before and after they were married, were also taken up with my mother's younger siblings. Alto and Gee were high school students at Fairfield when Mother and Daddy were teaching there. Because of the age difference, my parents helped raise them. Gee, sandy-haired, pretty, and spirited, was a handful and challenged her parents, particularly her mother, about everything from what dress to wear to what party to attend. Daddy was often a shoulder to cry on and a wise counselor, someone both my aunt and her parents trusted.

This was especially important when Gee abruptly left Spelman College in Atlanta without informing her parents. Gee, it seems, had decided to go to New York, where she planned to marry an Irish boy named Andy she had met there. Granddaddy Ray boarded a train and brought her back to Birmingham. My father, sensing that Gee could not at that moment live at home, arranged for her to go to Norfolk, Virginia, and live with his sister and mother. She attended and graduated from Norfolk State University, where Aunt Theresa was a faculty member. Gee became a teacher and later principal at a school for children with special needs.

Daddy was also very close to Mother's brother Alto. He was unable to convince Alto to play football—Alto said that being hit once was enough for him—but the two became like brothers. Alto was incredibly handsome, with dark, wavy hair and an athletic build. As Gee would later do, he started college but soon quit. He joined the army, where he used his extraordinary talents as a trumpeter to play in the band throughout Europe and admittedly avoid the hard work of infantry duty.

That wasn't good enough for my grandfather, who was determined to see every one of his children get a college education. After selling insurance for a while, Alto was shipped off to Southern University in Baton Rouge, Louisiana. Alto finished college and, like most of the Rays, became a teacher.

Thus, like most of their middle-class peers in segregated Birmingham, John and Angelena managed to live full and productive lives. Segregation provided in some ways a kind of buffer in which they could, for the most part, control their environment. Like their friends and neighbors, my parents kept their distance from the white world and created a relatively placid cocoon of family, church, community, and school.

But when my parents did have to venture outside of their narrow world, shocking things happened. My uncle tells the story of the night that my father drove him back to college in Louisiana after a holiday at home. Their car broke down on a dark back road. That was in the days when a sign at the Louisiana border was said to have read, "Run, nigger, run! If you don't know how to read, run anyway." A highway patrolman came upon them and asked why they were there. They explained that their car had broken down. "All right," he said. "But you boys had better have your black asses out of here before I come back." By the light of the matches my father had with him, Alto, a master auto mechanic, somehow found a way to get the car started. The two young black men were grateful to be gone before the officer returned.

Another oft-told family story relates to my father's decision to become a Republican. Daddy and Mother went to register to vote one day in 1952. Back then Southern officials frequently used poll tests as a way to discourage black people from voting. Mother sailed through the poll test after the clerk said to the pretty, light-skinned Angelena, "You surely know who the first President of the United States was, don't you?"

"Yes," Mother answered, "George Washington."

But when my dark-skinned father stepped forward, the clerk pointed to a container filled with hundreds of beans. "How many beans are in this jar?" he asked my father. They were obviously impossible to count.

Daddy was devastated and related his experience to an elder in his church, Mr. Frank Hunter. The old man told him not to worry; he knew how to get him registered. In those days, Alabama was Democrat country. The term "yellow dog Democrat," as in "I'd rather vote for a yellow dog than a Republican," was often used during this era. "There's one clerk down there who is Republican and is trying to build the party," Mr. Hunter told my father. "She'll register anybody who'll say they're Republican." Daddy went down, found the woman, and successfully registered. He never forgot that and for the rest of his life was a faithful member of the Republican Party.

chapter six

Finally, after almost three years, my parents were married on February 12, 1954. Daddy was thirty and Mother twenty-nine, relatively old to be tying the knot in those days. Whenever I asked what had taken them so long, neither had a really good answer. I did not know until after my mother died in 1985 that my father had been married before. The woman had apparently told my father that she was pregnant when she was not. That experience likely prevented my father from wanting to jump quickly back into marriage.

At the time that Daddy married Mother, he was fully immersed in his pastoral responsibilities at Westminster Presbyterian Church in Birmingham. Granddaddy had chartered the church in 1944, but by 1952 he had resigned and moved to Mississippi with my grandmother, trying to revive a troubled congregation there. Westminster's new sanctuary had been completed and the church formally accepted into the presbytery by the beginning of my father's leadership. Maybe he just decided that it was time to settle down.

So with both approving sets of parents present and Granddaddy Rice officiating, John and Angelena married in her parents' music room on February 12. Theresa, Alto, and Gee were the only others present. Mother wore a gray suit and spectacular smoke-gray shoes with rhinestones on them. The wedding had to be squeezed in between Daddy's basketball game and an oratorical contest awards ceremony at which Gee was receiving a scholarship. After the awards ceremony, Daddy returned home to the church and Mother spent the night at her parents'. She moved into the back of the church with her new husband the next day.

Life wasn't so easy for the young bride, who became the church congregation's new center of attention. Being a preacher's wife ensures one of great scrutiny. And to be fair, Mother didn't always exhibit much warmth with people outside of her family. There was also some jealousy, particularly from the mothers of marriageable-aged daughters in the congregation who'd hoped the young preacher might become their son-in-law.

It probably didn't help that the young couple lived literally in the back of the church. The little apartment consisted of a bedroom, kitchen, and bathroom connected by a small hallway to a living room next to the pastor's office. Privacy was at a premium. The church members had treated the living room as common space before my mother moved in. They loved to gather after the service, particularly when inclement weather drove them inside.

When my mother moved in and furnished the place with

very nice mahogany pieces, bought on time at Sokol's furniture store, she put an end to the Sunday gatherings—or tried to, at least. When members refused to honor her decision, Mother covered her nice sofa in plastic and bought cheap chairs for the living room. A minor scandal erupted in the church as members excoriated Angelena for "not wanting them to sit on her furniture." In retrospect I'm glad she was so protective of those pieces, because I am now fortunate enough to own them.

In time, the congregation and Angelena began to make their peace. She stopped playing for Baptist churches and became the choir director at Westminster, which had been in dire need of one. Mother insisted that the church purchase an organ, which they did with the help of the Forbeses, a white family who owned the music store downtown and who adored my father. She formed a children's choir and started to direct holiday programs, endearing her to parents with school-age kids. And soon my parents announced that Mother was pregnant and that the child was due in November. It is a good thing that I was not born early. The arithmetic worked well enough—nine months and two days—to prevent wagging tongues among nosy church elders.

My parents' marriage created one other complication. The school system had a rule that barred spouses from teaching at the same place. Daddy left the Fairfield system and got a job as a guidance counselor at Ullman High School in the Birmingham school district. Mother stayed at Fairfield. I once asked Daddy how they had made that decision at a time when the woman would have been expected to give up her job, not the man. He simply said that Mother had been there longer and it was only fair that he move. I still think that it was a very enlightened decision for that era.

My parents planned to stay in the back of the church because there wasn't really enough money to move. But Daddy convinced the congregation to paint the bedroom and bath, and Mother bought stuffed animals and a baby book to record every important event.

Tragically, these happy preparations were interrupted by the sudden death of Granddaddy Rice. Daddy and Alto had just made one of their periodic visits to my grandparents in Mississippi, and right when they returned home, Daddy received a phone call from his mother. Granddaddy Rice had suffered a heart attack. They got back in the car and raced to Mississippi.

When they arrived, Granddaddy Rice was already dead, but my grandmother had been too shocked to do anything with the body, which was still lying on the floor. My father and uncle arranged to have Granddaddy's body brought back to Birmingham. A grand funeral was held for this exceptional man at Westminster Presbyterian, the last congregation that he had founded. My mother, seven months pregnant, played the organ, and my father officiated. The church was packed with people who had come from as far away as Louisiana.

My grandfather had been a giant in so many people's lives and in our family lore. He managed to get his college education and to educate his own children and many others as well. He never let anything get in the way of providing an intellectual environment for his family or pursuing the development of his own mind. My father told me a story that seemed to sum up my grandfather's passion for learning. One day Granddaddy Rice came home very excited about a new purchase. It was during the Great Depression, and my grandmother was trying hard to manage on their meager resources. Yet there was Granddaddy with nine leather-bound, gold-embossed books: the works of Hugo, Shakespeare, Balzac, and others. Each book began with a summary essay about the author and his work. My grandmother asked how much they had cost. Granddaddy Rice admitted they cost ninety dollars but told her not to worry because he had purchased them on time—they would only have to pay three dollars a month for the next *three years*. Grandmother was furious, but Granddaddy held his ground and refused to return the books. I am so grateful that he did not give in. One of the proudest days of my life was when my father gave me the surviving five volumes as I left for the ceremony to receive my PhD.

Granddaddy Rice died on September 14, precisely two months before I was born. I am told that he was thrilled when my mother became pregnant, saying that it would be really nice to have a child around the house. I deeply regret that I never knew him in the flesh, but I've always felt that I do know him in spirit. He has been a powerful guiding presence throughout my life. And I have those books: my bond with him. It is as if through them he has passed on to me the gift of transformation through education that he himself earned in the hardest of times and against very long odds.

chapter seven

My mother and father plunged into parenthood with a vengeance. Early on they sought to build a good learning environment for me, reading stories to me every night until I was able to read myself. My mother was as determined to raise a musician as my father was to cultivate a sports fan. She bought my first piano when I was three months old, and I learned later that we would "play" songs together, Mother moving my fingers along the little keyboard.

Before I was one my mother returned to teaching. There weren't any debates in my community about the relative merits of rearing children while working. Almost all of the women in my community worked, most as teachers. Teaching was such a prized profession that most who could teach did. There weren't many other options except perhaps nursing. Most men did the same, though occasionally they went to law or medical school.

Extended families provided a good child care alternative for these working parents. It was convenient that the length of the school day as well as vacations were roughly the same for parents who worked in the schools and for their children. But often grandparents filled in with kids who weren't yet school-age. I was dropped off by my parents at my maternal grandparents' house in the morning and picked up after school. There was no safer or more nurturing environment than the one provided by Grandmother and Granddaddy Ray.

When I was almost four, my father persuaded the church to build a proper manse so that we could move out of Westminster. I have only a few memories of living in the back of the church, but I remember very well the whole process of building the small gray house on a corner lot at 929 Center Way Southwest. The manse was located about five minutes from the church in Birmingham's black middle-class neighborhood of Titusville.

My parents tried to involve me in family decision making from a very young age, and the impending family move was a perfect opportunity. There were so many decisions to make about paint colors and the functions that would be assigned to various rooms. I personally picked the pale green for the bathroom, the yellow for the kitchen, and a rich blue for my playroom. Mother decided on "Chinese red" for the living room. Since I was an only child and had no competition from siblings for space, I had a pink bedroom in addition to the playroom. But I was afraid to sleep in it alone, having shared the bedroom in the church with my parents. My bedroom was soon turned into a small den and a second bed was put in my parents' room. This was the arrangement for a few years until at about eight I declared the need for my own space and reclaimed my bedroom.

But then there was the question of what to do for a den. Again here was an opportunity to involve me in decision making. By now I was president of the family. We held an election every year. My father insisted on a secret ballot, but since my mother always voted for me I was assured of victory. There were no term limits. My responsibilities included calling family meetings to decide matters such as departure times for trips, plans for decorating the house at Christmas, and other issues related to daily life. So I called a meeting, and after some discussion we all agreed that the playroom should become the den.

The move to 929 Center Way had been one of the most exciting times in our lives and included the family's first TV purchase, a little thirteen-inch Zenith black-and-white set. We watched a lot of TV. I have many intellectual friends who either don't watch TV or pretend that they don't. Some go so far as to refuse to own one. And I know that parents today restrict television watching for their kids.

My parents didn't set limits on how much TV I watched. To be fair, television was a lot more wholesome in the late 1950s. But there was more to it than that. I have always thought that it's harder to be the parent of an only child than to be an only child. Someone has to entertain the little one when night falls and playmates go home. In that regard, television was one of my parents' best friends. We watched TV together just about every night, and I often watched alone too.

The only black people regularly on TV were the characters on *Amos 'n' Andy*, and while we watched their antics, my parents went out of their way to point out and correct their butchered English. Mostly I watched cartoons such as *Popeye* and situation comedies such as *I Love Lucy*. *The Popeye Show* took place in a studio with Cousin Cliff, a big white man in a sailor suit, hosting an audience of schoolkids. Sometimes kids would bring their friends and celebrate a birthday on TV. The studio audience was all white, of course, until about 1962, when the show started devoting a few days each year to "Negro day." I actually got to go when I was about seven years old and one of my friends had her birthday party there. I remember finding the whole highly anticipated event rather disappointing. We drove up to Red Mountain, where Channel 13 was located, sat on bleachers in a studio, and went home. I never again held Cousin Cliff in high esteem.

My mother also made sure that I watched *Mighty Mouse*, in which the heroic mouse sang, "Here I come to save the day!" Mother explained that this was a form of opera in which dialogue is sung, not spoken. She seemed to find high culture in just about everything.

But my favorite show was *The Mickey Mouse Club*, which we watched as a family every day after school. All three of us would put on our mouse ears and sing, "M-I-C (See you real soon) . . . K-E-Y (Why? Because we like you) . . . M-O-U-S-E." It was a real family ritual, not to be interrupted by anything. One day Mr. Binham the insurance agent was in the living room pitching my parents on some new policy. He was the only white man I can ever remember coming into our house in Titusville. In any case, it was about time to sing the Mickey Mouse song, and I was becoming agitated that my parents were otherwise occupied. Daddy politely told Mr. Binham that he'd have to wait. We put on our mouse ears and engaged in our family ritual. I felt very proud that my parents had put our time above whatever business it was they had with Mr. Binham. This small gesture was simply one of the many that communicated they always had time for me.

After *The Mickey Mouse Club* we would take a break from television for reading time and, as I became older, doing homework together. We would then tune into the nationally televised news program *The Huntley-Brinkley Report*. My father would comment on each story, explaining the historical significance of big events. I remember watching John Glenn's historic mission to space, which preempted all other programming for the entire mission. For a while I wanted to be an astronaut, as did most of my friends. We'd load up our "space capsule" out in the backyard, with some lucky kid getting to be the astronaut and others being confined to earth as ground controllers.

But one of my most vivid childhood memories is the Cuban missile crisis in October 1962, in which the United States and the Soviet Union engaged in a tense standoff over the placement of Soviet missiles in Cuba. We were glued to the set every evening during those thirteen days. It was a very scary time. We'd never bothered with a bomb shelter in the house, even at the height of the Cold War. But some of our friends did have them, fully stocked with provisions to survive a nuclear exchange. In school, we went through duck-and-cover drills. When the alarm sounded all the children fell to the floor, huddling under their desks. My friends and

I even played bomb shelter, crawling into the little space just beneath the house in response to a "nuclear attack."

But the crisis in Cuba was no drill. Because the missiles would have been deployed just ninety miles from the Florida coast, the newscasters reported, probably incorrectly, that Birmingham was in range. They showed big arrows pointing right at us. I could tell that my father was worried, and I realized that this was something my parents couldn't save me from. It was the first time that I remember feeling truly vulnerable.

Daddy explained that our country had never lost a war, and he was sure we weren't going to lose this one. He was nevertheless visibly relieved when the Soviet ships turned around, ending the crisis. The whole episode had a surprisingly strong impact on me. I once told an audience of Cuban Americans that Fidel Castro had put the United States at risk in allowing those missiles to be deployed. "He should pay for it until he dies," I said. Even I was surprised by the rawness of that comment.

chapter eight

After our move to 929 Center Way, my parents set about building a solid and enjoyable life for our family. Each day my father would drop me off at my grandparents' and Mother and Daddy would come together after school to pick me up. Granddaddy still worked a pretty full day, and my grandmother was a full-time homemaker. I'd "help" her around the house and watch soap operas with her. She loved *As the World Turns*, and I loved the commercials, especially for Tide and Mr. Clean, which made stains disappear right before your very eyes.

Sometimes Daddy would pick me up early to go to a high school football game at Rickwood Field, the somewhat dilapidated stadium at which black high school teams played their games. According to Grandmother, I would become so excited at the prospect of going to a game that I would pester her all day about the time. "When is it going to be two

o'clock?" I would ask over and over. My exasperated grandmother finally showed me a clock and the position of the
hands at two o'clock so that I could track the time myself. I
guess I can thank football for helping me learn how to tell
time.

But the activity that I enjoyed most was watching my
grandmother teach piano. Grandmother Ray had about
twenty students, ranging from beginners to quite advanced
pianists. Her lessons started at about three o'clock every day,
and she taught for a couple of hours, charging twenty-five
cents a session. When the students would leave I'd go to the
piano and pretend to play, banging at the keys and "reading"
the music. Then I'd ask to take some sheet music home so I
could "practice." Each day I'd leave with music, usually for-
getting to bring it back the next day. To preserve her music
collection, Grandmother finally gave me a regular book to
take home. "Grandmother, this isn't music!" I told her.

Grandmother Ray decided that it was unusual for a kid to
know the difference and asked my mother if she could start
giving me piano lessons. I was three years old, and they wondered if it might be too early but decided to give it a try. Unlike the early experiment with first grade, this worked. I loved
the piano.

Grandmother started every student with books of exercises that trained young fingers to do progressively more difficult things. Each student also learned a prescribed series of
increasingly more difficult hymns, starting with "What a
Friend We Have in Jesus." My parents had bought a little
electronic organ for our new house, and I'd play for hours
when we got home. They claimed that it was hard to get me

to do anything else, including read books or watch television. But a problem emerged as I began to play hymns: the little organ did not have enough keys. Each time I wanted to play low notes, I was out of luck.

"I need a piano," I told my parents several months into my lessons.

Daddy made me a deal. "When you can play 'What a Friend We Have in Jesus' perfectly, we will buy you a piano," he said.

The next day I went to my grandmother's and sat at the piano for eight hours, not even wanting to break for lunch. I practiced and practiced, and when my parents came to pick me up I played "What a Friend" *perfectly*!

As they'd do many times in my life, John and Angelena found a way not to disappoint. They didn't have the money to buy a piano, but they rented one the next day from Forbes Piano Company. By the end of the week I had a brand-new Wurlitzer spinet.

I became good at the piano very quickly and started to play publicly. Mother found opportunities for me to play at various church functions as well as citywide events. I played several pieces at the gathering of new teachers in 1959, where I was decked out in a gray polished cotton dress with pink flowers, black patent shoes with rhinestones, and a white fur hat. I don't remember being nervous and have always thought that these early experiences helped me to overcome any sense of stage fright.

My mother reinforced my inclination toward music in multiple ways. She'd buy books written for children about the great composers. I imagined what it would have been like to meet Beethoven, who scribbled musical notations on tablecloths, or Bach, who fathered twenty children. My favorite story was about Mozart's life. I was totally enchanted by this man who had written so much and died so young, at the age of thirty-five. I even developed a little crush on him, imagining myself as his wife, Constanze. Admittedly, this was a strange infatuation for a little black girl in Birmingham. Most of my friends were in love with Elvis Presley.

Mother also brought home records, which we would listen to together. One day, when I was about five years old, she brought home *Aïda*, the Giuseppe Verdi opera. My little eyes were as big as saucers as I listened to the "Triumphal March" for the first time, and I played the record over and over. And on Saturdays we listened to radio broadcasts of the New York Metropolitan Opera, "brought to you by Texaco." Opera and classical music were totally and completely my mother's domain. My father loved jazz but had no interest in or taste for classical music. Even so, he displayed admirable patience when my mother and I took charge of what was playing on the car radio as we ran errands on Saturday afternoon.

Daddy did teach me to dance. He'd put on a record by jazz singer Dinah Washington or play the big-band music of performers such as Duke Ellington. Then I would stand on his feet as he walked me through the box step or the fox-trot.

But Daddy's real territory was sports, and I took to it with great fervor. We watched the National Football League on television every Sunday after church. In those days, there was one game and no halftime studio show. Daddy wanted me to really understand football and would analyze the plays, explaining what the defense was doing to counter the offense and vice versa.

Our team was the Cleveland Browns, and to this day I am a fan. This may seem puzzling given that I didn't visit Cleveland until the mid-1990s. The reason is simple: Birmingham had no NFL team when I was a child. It was one of only two cities in the South, the other being Memphis, that prohibited blacks and whites from playing together professionally. But even in other southern cities, black players had trouble finding hotels to stay in and restaurants to eat in. By the late 1950s, the NFL was refusing to play in the South at all because of segregation.

The last team to integrate was the Washington Redskins, which had no black players until 1962. Though Washington, D.C., was geographically the closest to us, my father hated the Redskins for their racist policies. They couldn't be our team. So we rooted for the Cleveland Browns, who had the great black running back Jim Brown. And each Thanksgiving, Daddy and I would watch the Detroit Lions, who by tradition played on that holiday every year. The next day, we would play the "Rice Bowl," a touch football game held at "Rice Stadium," known the rest of the year as the front yard.

chapter nine

My parents may have doted on their only child a little more than their friends, but they shared the same goals of other parents to provide a safe, nurturing, and stimulating environment for their kids. The task was hard and complex, yet straightforward at the same time. The hard part was obvious: Birmingham was the most segregated big city in America, and daily life was full of demeaning reminders of the second-class citizenship accorded to blacks. Whites and blacks lived in parallel worlds, their paths crossing uneasily in only a few public places.

So how can I say that there was a straightforward way for black parents to nurture their children? Well, ironically, because Birmingham was so segregated, black parents were able, in large part, to control the environment in which they raised their children. They rigorously regulated the messages that we received and shielded us by imposing high expectations and a determined insistence on excellence. It took a lot of energy for our parents to channel us in the right direction, but we became neither dispirited nor bitter.

The extended family, including grandparents, aunts, uncles, and cousins, provided the first layer of support and nurture. The community mentors were not far outside the family circle, and our little neighborhood of Titusville provided a strong network of black professionals who were determined to prepare their kids for productive lives. There were few single parents, and black men were a dominant presence in the community.

The schools too were completely segregated in Birmingham—there were no white teachers, no white students. Education in Alabama was well behind the rest of the country. For a number of years schools did not provide free textbooks to any student, black or white. Although my parents bought mine, some of my classmates were often forced to share one book. Sometimes teachers would pool their money to buy a few extras for their classes. The city put fewer resources into the black schools, so they were substandard in an already poor state system. But the teachers were dedicated, and they produced remarkable results. In these circumstances, teachers could demand the best of their students without any racial overtones. Teachers had high expectations and were pretty tough on low performers. "To succeed," they routinely reminded us, "you will have to be twice as good." This was declared as a matter of fact, not a point for debate.

The churches provided a final pillar of support. There was no question as to where you should be on Sunday morning. There were no atheists and no agnostics in my middle-class community. The two largest churches, Sixth Avenue and Sixteenth Street, were Baptist.

Birmingham's churches were competitive with each other for members and vied for the reputation of having the most compelling services and outstanding music. It also helped to have influential members, particularly those lured away from other congregations. But the churches were more than a place to worship on Sundays. They were also the locus of much of the community's social life and safe places for kids. Later, some would also become centers of political mobilization.

All of these elements—extended family, community, schools, and churches—conspired together to convince me and my peers that racism was "their" problem, not ours. Whatever feelings of insecurity or inadequacy black adults felt in the appalling and depressing circumstances of Jim Crow Birmingham, they did not transfer it to us. For the children of our little enclave, Titusville, the message was crystal clear: *We love you and will give you everything we can to help you succeed. But there are no excuses and there is no place for victims.*

chapter ten

While I grew up in this larger environment of family, church, community, and school, my circumstances were special because I was an only child. My parents were sensitive to this and strove to make sure that I had plenty of contact with other children. Apparently, I didn't want siblings. Mother told me that I asked repeatedly whether she intended to have any more kids, making clear that I would not be supportive of that decision. Most likely my parents just decided that one was enough, since at the time of my birth Mother was already older by the standards of the day.

In lieu of siblings, I had several close friends, including Vanessa Hunter, Margaret Wright, and Carole Smitherman. I was also close to my cousins Lativia, Yvonne, and Albert. Even after Uncle Albert and his family moved to take up a congregation in Thomasville, Georgia, our families made certain to pay each other holiday and summer visits.

When I was about to turn five, my parents decided that it would be good to enroll me in kindergarten. Throughout my childhood, Mother always contended that I was well adjusted and got along well with other kids. My father, though, felt I was not at ease with other kids, and enrolling me in kindergarten became one of his many attempts over the years to make sure that I was competent socially. I struggled at times, exhibiting a bit of a thin skin and a tendency to retaliate when I felt slighted by my friends.

Once when I was seven my neighborhood friends decided not to invite me to play with them for a couple of days in a row. I always had the latest dolls. I loved to line them up and "teach" them, especially my favorite doll, Baby Dear, who was a very good student. So on the third day I gathered up all of my dolls and took them out to the front lawn, where, in view of my little friends, I began to play. When my friends came over, I informed them that I really didn't have time to spend with them, that they were at my house and these were my dolls, and they should go home. My father said that he watched with pride but also with a bit of horror. On one hand, I proved able to stand up for myself in a pretty clever way. On the other, he told me, it wasn't always good to try to get back at people, though he understood why I was hurt by what they had done. My friends and I eventually made up, of course, and years later my parents and I laughed about the incident. I told my father that I had received his message— but I also noted that my friends hadn't ever done that to me again.

In any event, with an eye toward reining in my less sociable tendencies, my parents began in 1959 to look for a good kindergarten in which to enroll me. The school system didn't have kindergarten classes, but there were a few private alternatives; in fact, my father's church had sponsored a kindergarten a couple of years earlier. Daddy decided to restart the program and recruited a retired teacher, Mrs. Evelyn Hunter, to teach the children. Mrs. Hunter was a member of Westminster and the widow of Frank Hunter, who'd helped my father register to vote in 1952.

The kindergarten program was largely academic, emphasizing reading, writing, and arithmetic. But there were also lots of fun activities as well, including stickball and singing. I loved kindergarten and eagerly went every day. I was a chubby little kid and sometimes bore the brunt of teasing about it. My head was kind of big, and some little kid started calling me "watermelon head." I retaliated with a comeback that I can't remember now, but in general, I got along better than expected with my classmates.

Florissa Lewis was my best friend in kindergarten. She remained so even after an incident that could have ended our friendship early. At the Easter program at church we were each assigned to deliver a speech. Mine was "Ring, Easter bells. Ring, ring, ring. Tell the glad tidings of Christ the risen King." Florissa was supposed to follow with her own part. I don't remember the words now, but I did on that day. When Florissa hesitated, I started delivering her speech too. My parents and hers were thoroughly embarrassed, but I thought I was just helping out.

After a year, we "graduated" from kindergarten in a ceremony complete with white robes and diplomas held in the church sanctuary. All of the other kids were on their way to first grade, but I wasn't. I was very sensitive about this and didn't want the other children to know. The problem was that I would not turn six until November, too late to meet the October 31 cutoff set by the school system.

My parents were determined to see that I not miss an entire year of school. They tried to get the school system to count my time in kindergarten and let me test into first grade. The Board of Education would not budge, so they came up with another idea. Perhaps I could test into second grade the following year. Having received permission for this unusual maneuver, they set about making certain that I would pass the test.

My mother decided to take a year's leave from teaching to coach me in preparation for the exam. Years later when the homeschooling movement became more visible, I belatedly realized that I had been a part of it, if only in an ad hoc way. Mother was very systematic about my school day. We'd get up and see Daddy off to work and then start "school." She ordered the first- and second-grade texts in math, science, and reading and took me through them in a very rigorous fashion. I'd take tests every week to chart our progress. This flexible schedule also allowed time to practice piano, and as a result, I advanced significantly during this period.

Occasionally, if I did well in my schoolwork, we would knock off a little early and go shopping in downtown Birmingham. One such trip yielded my first Barbie doll, dressed in the iconic black and white zebra-striped bathing suit. But for the most part, my mother was all business and very demanding.

I didn't mind having my mother teach me at home,

except for one thing: I wanted to be like the other kids, who would go to school every morning and come home at the end of the day. I felt so different, and I hated it. So I invented a story that I was going to another school outside the community. Each morning as the kids were leaving, I'd get my books and go outside, pretending to wait for a ride to school. When they returned, I'd "come home." This subterfuge didn't last long because the other kids began to ask too many questions about my other school. My parents didn't particularly like this deception, including the desire to "fit in," and convinced me that I had to tell the truth. So I admitted to my friends that I was studying at home. "Next year," I proclaimed, "I will be in second grade!" I was very proud when I passed the test, scoring at a third-grade level in arithmetic and at a fifth-grade level in reading. I entered Lane Elementary School as a six-year-old second grader.

Though my neighborhood school was Center Street Elementary, I was enrolled in Lane Elementary because it was across the street from Ullman High, where Daddy worked. He would drop me off and then, at the end of the shorter elementary school day, leave work early and pick me up. After that I'd stay with him, doing my homework in his office (he was the guidance counselor) and getting to know the "big kids."

After launching me academically, Mother returned to work. Each morning she'd carpool to school with other teachers. She had received a credential to teach science and was assigned to Western-Olin High School. Parker High School was the flagship black school, located in mostly middle-class Smithfield. Ullman High School was the other prized place to work, located a few blocks from our house in middle-class Titusville.

Western-Olin was located in Ensley, squarely in the middle of steel-mill country and known as tough territory. The students were mostly from the publicly run housing projects, and violence inside and outside of school was frequent. Even in those days there were a fair number of single mothers and children being raised by grandparents. Ensley was not considered a desirable place to work. I remember my father's concern about Mother working in such a tough environment.

Western-Olin was one of two schools that had a divided curriculum. Some students attended Western, the academic high school, full-time, while others would complete a half day of academics and spend the balance of the afternoon in vocational programs at Olin. The campuses were in the same place, but it was as if the students lived in parallel universes. The vocational school students were seldom encouraged to even think of attending college; they were just expected to acquire minimal competence in reading and arithmetic and then specialize in a skill such as cosmetology or auto mechanics.

Mother believed that the vocational kids weren't taken seriously enough and that this, in part, produced the behavior problems that were so prevalent. She went out of her way to serve these kids, making some her "assistants" and giving them tasks such as cleaning the science lab so that they'd feel their contributions were valued. She would then make sure that they received certificates at graduation. These kids likely would have received no honors at graduation but for those that my mother invented. I remember one student in particular, a young woman who was tall and heavyset with dyed flaming-red hair, who had built a track record of chronic behavioral issues. Each day she would come to work for Mother, eventually becoming trusted enough to open and close the science lab with her own key. She and my mother cried when she graduated, having beaten the odds that were so clearly stacked against her.

Mother also believed that the arts could make a difference for these kids and for this underprivileged community as a whole. In 1962 she decided to produce a full-scale operetta with the students. The kids performed *Chenita*, which used Franz Liszt's music to tell the story of a Gypsy family. The next year they were much more ambitious and performed George Gershwin's *Porgy and Bess*.

Rehearsals would start just after Christmas for a performance in the spring. Parents were required to buy the material for the costumes, which were made in sewing classes. If a student couldn't afford the fabric, the teachers pitched in and purchased it. The scenery was made in the carpentry shop.

These events were always exciting for my family. As the production approached, Mother was at the school almost every evening, and I would often go to the rehearsals. Aunt Connie, who was also a teacher at Western-Olin, assisted my mother. The shows were on Friday and Saturday nights, and I got to take Friday off from school to help Mother with the final preparations. Parents, grandparents, students, and the rest of the community would show up for the performance, dressed in their finest as if they were attending the Metropolitan Opera.

My mother's productions were more elaborate than most but not unlike what was going on throughout the Birmingham public schools. These segregated schools were determined to provide these kinds of opportunities to develop their students' artistic talents. The centerpiece of these efforts was the role of instrumental music and band. Today everyone marvels at the extraordinary band performances of historically black colleges such as Grambling or Florida A&M. This tradition ultimately traces its roots, however, to the commitment of elementary schools in the segregated South to early band instruction.

Band was an important part of the school day. In addition to attending a formal class period, band members would practice after school during both the marching band season in the fall and the concert season in the spring. I joined the Lane Elementary School band. Obviously, there was no place for a pianist in a marching band, so my parents suggested the bells (also called the glockenspiel), which had the advantage of being very much like playing the piano using a mallet. I wasn't convinced until my father told me that the bells could be heard above every other instrument in the band.

With the bands, the excellent choirs and glee clubs, plays, and variety shows, students in Birmingham's black schools had many opportunities to perform. No one saw these activities as extracurricular or add-ons. They were an essential part of transforming students into more cultured people with well-developed artistic talents.

The performances were also occasions for the community to come together. A play or concert at one of the high schools was a highly anticipated social event. So too were the periodic visits of acclaimed choirs and bands from the historically black colleges. The best-known choir was the Fisk Jubilee Singers, but almost every college had one. We'd travel to Stillman College in Tuscaloosa for special performances from artists such as the great black opera singer Marian Anderson in 1964. These activities were a key part of our social life at a time when it wasn't possible to go to a concert downtown or even to a proper movie theater. They were an important and satisfying element of our parallel universe in segregated Birmingham.

chapter eleven

The other great social outlet was the church. My father's church, Westminster Presbyterian, was centrally located on Sixth Avenue not very far from downtown Birmingham. The neighborhood was solidly middle-class, and this was reflected in its congregation.

Services were formal and short, no more than an hour. Black Presbyterian services were a world apart from the emotional and high-energy services of the Baptist churches. Gospel music was rare, and there was no "call and response," where the preacher would say, for instance, "Do you hear me?" and the congregation would reply, "I hear you." There wasn't even a stray "Amen." I don't mean to make the services sound boring. In fact, they were beautiful, even inspiring.

The Christmas and Easter holidays were particularly busy and enjoyable, celebrated with plays for the children and special music that took months to prepare. I loved to go to the church and help decorate, particularly on Easter, when the altar was adorned with three crosses that my uncle Alto built in his shop. There was a glorious sunrise service at six o'clock and then the regular one at eleven.

I didn't care much, though, for the Easter egg hunt the Saturday before. I thought it was kind of pointless to hide eggs and then try to find them. I was particularly put off when I caught my parents putting an egg in my basket so that I would not be embarrassed if I failed to find one. I asked them to stop doing that, protesting that I was smart enough to find a stupid egg if I wanted to. I just didn't want to.

My father was a terrific preacher, though he rarely raised his voice above a normal speaking tone. "He was known as a pastor who made you think before you could feel," to quote one of his elders. This "lecture style" of preaching brought in many new members, particularly teachers who identified with my father's more cerebral approach to his ministry.

From the time I was very young I loved to engage in theological debates with my father. This started at the age of four, when I insisted that my father was mispronouncing the name Job. It was pronounced "Job," I insisted, not "Jobe"! My father, ever tolerant of my dissent, argued patiently and I guess decided that eventually I would know better. Our theological debates became a bit more sophisticated over the years. I always felt that my father wanted me to use my intellect to help build my faith. I was never told to simply accept anything on the face of it, and my constant questions were always engaged. Because my father never made reason and faith enemies of each other, my religious conviction was strengthened. I am grateful for that because in the many intellectual environs in which I have found myself, I have never suffered the crisis of faith that so many do. I have always *believed*, fully and completely.

Westminster grew rapidly under Daddy's leadership, with new members joining frequently. He knew that it was important to make his church more than just a place of worship on Sunday. Most churches had a social component, but Daddy's church was ahead of its time, providing a place to gather all week long. Choir practice was on Wednesdays, Bible study on Thursdays, and on Tuesdays and Thursdays, church members who were teachers offered tutoring in algebra, science, and foreign languages. Dr. Duval, a white dentist, would come to the church once a month to conduct checkups and perform dental work. There were also typing classes and etiquette lessons that taught young people such things as which fork to use at the dinner table. Friday night was "flop night," a time when kids could come to the church for everything from chess lessons to movies, watched on a projector borrowed from the school. In the summer we looked forward to church-sponsored cookouts, as well as volleyball matches and track meets.

These activities were open to the whole community, not just to the church members. This was somewhat controversial, particularly when Daddy insisted on including the kids from Loveman Village, the government housing project behind the church. There was considerable class stratification in segregated black Birmingham. I remember being told by my mother, for instance, that my friends from Lane Elementary could come to visit me but I could not go to visit them. Their neighborhood was "too rough."

Many of our church members were not comfortable with Daddy's outreach activities. I recall one attempt at inclusion that backfired when during a picnic some of the kids from Loveman Village were caught teaching children from the congregation to shoot craps behind the church. "Reverend Rice, I told you they weren't ready to be with us," an elder told my father. Daddy came home and told Mother about the episode. He was really hurt and defended his program. But he was always struggling to reconcile his desire for the broadest outreach with what his church's middle-class membership would tolerate.

Relations were sometimes very strained when my father pushed church members beyond their comfort zone. At one meeting of the Board of Elders, the powerful governing committee in Presbyterian churches, members decided to deny money for Daddy's "missionary work." My father became so angry that he turned over a table and stormed out. Daddy was a big man and could be physical in his expression of anger, though never with my mother or with me.

Daddy decided to seek support among the women of the church, getting the Presbyterian Women's Circle to fund his activities. His stalwart supporters shared his vision of the centrality of a ministry for children—everybody's children. Daddy, in turn, tried to get the presbytery to ordain these women as elders. When the Presbyterian Church of the late 1950s refused to do so, he created a special category for them. They were allowed, for instance, to serve communion, likely in violation of church policy. He didn't ask permission, and in the end, no one objected.

My father's somewhat controversial youth ministry became central to Westminster. The links between the church and the community were nurtured through the Youth Fellowship program and the club that Daddy formed for teenage boys, the Cavaliers. They wore yellow hats with "Cavaliers" written in purple across the front. Daddy involved several other men from the church and the community in what is now called mentoring.

Youth Fellowship met every Sunday afternoon at four in the church, with social activities for high school kids. My father and a parishioner named Miss Julia Emma Smith arranged panel discussions, tutoring sessions, and a one-week summer leadership conference at Stillman College. Daddy wanted the kids to know that there was a bigger and different world outside of their immediate environment. He befriended a rabbi and on Sundays took his students to Temple Beth-El and Temple Emanu-El to learn about Judaism through lectures arranged specifically for them. The young people of Westminster also participated in an "exchange" program with a large white church, South Highland Presbyterian, during the early 1960s, when segregation was still almost total. The minister and my father decided to do this despite trepidation on the part of both congregations. It appears that the exchanges happened only a few times, likely owing to growing opposition in the congregations.

In addition to these educational and cultural opportunities, my father could also provide something that the Baptists couldn't: dances and parties. Some members complained that the church should not be used for dances. Daddy countered that the church was the safest possible place for kids to have their parties. Moreover, parents trusted him, and the dances he arranged were always heavily attended. One night some of the kids decided to hold a house party and tell their parents that Reverend Rice would be there, which was not true. When Daddy found out just before the party was to take place, he went to the students and told them to recant their story or he would go individually to their parents and explain the truth. I rode in the car with him as he confronted each student. Playing the role of a vindictive little sister, I lobbied to have him tell their parents. Daddy refused, saying that it was important that the students come clean themselves. He left it to the parents to discipline their children. He never had that problem again.

In fact, Youth Fellowship and the Cavaliers were vehicles for my father's educational evangelism. Much like his father before him, he would insist on strong academic performance and counsel each student toward college. Daddy's "kids" turned out to be a remarkable lot. For example, Freeman Hrabowski III (a black teenager apparently with Polish ancestry) lived at the corner of our street. My father called him his "little math genius." Freeman went to college at fifteen, received a PhD in higher education administration and statistics, and now serves as president of the University of Maryland, Baltimore County, where he became well known for his pioneering work in inspiring young black students, particularly men, to pursue careers in math and the sciences. Sheryl McCarthy, who once wrote and delivered a "newscast" of the crucifixion on Good Friday, went on to become an award-winning journalist at *Newsday* and the *New York Daily News*, as well as a national correspondent for ABC News. Amelia Rutledge, studious and quiet, was the valedictorian at Ullman, eventually earned a PhD in medieval studies from Yale, and now teaches at George Mason University. Larry Naves, a member of the Cavaliers, became chief judge for the Denver District Court in Colorado. Mary Kate Bush finished Fisk magna cum laude, received an MBA from the University of Chicago, and became a Treasury official in the Reagan administration, as well as the first black woman to serve as the United States government's representative on the board of the International Monetary Fund. Carole Smitherman served as president of the Birmingham City Council and became the first black woman to serve as a circuit court judge in Alabama.

These were the children of middle-class Titusville. But the success stories extended to less-advantaged kids. Gloria Dennard became director of library media services at the Jefferson County Board of Education. I cried at Daddy's memorial service when Gloria said that but for my father's intervention with her parents, who were not college-educated, she would never have gone on to college. Barbara S. Allen, who served as interim superintendent of the Birmingham public schools, also says that it was my father who insisted that she get a degree. And Harold Jackson, a Pulitzer Prize–winning journalist and editorial editor at the *Philadelphia Inquirer*, was a Youth Fellowship kid. Harold credited Daddy for laying the spiritual foundation for his life and inspiring his older siblings to pursue a college education.

These were just a few of the scores of teachers, doctors,

lawyers, and other professionals who grew up at that time in deeply segregated Birmingham. They clearly took the right messages from their parents, teachers, and mentors like my father and mother, who emphasized excellence and hard work and never tolerated victimhood. And these future professionals were, in turn, role models for younger kids like me.

Over the years, I have come to understand that it must have been much tougher for these older kids to stay focused and positive. I was very young in segregated Birmingham and perhaps easier to insulate from its negative influences. But these teenagers were well aware of their circumstances. They must have felt the sense of injustice and harm more intensely than those of us who were younger. That they still succeeded and internalized the positive messages of their teachers and parents is a great testament to their focus and perseverance.

chapter twelve

Because I so wanted to emulate the older kids, my parents found it rather easy to discipline me. I can only remember being spanked once. That was when I ignored my parents' order not to climb up on a chair to get my Halloween costume from the top shelf of the closet and almost fell. Usually, though, they only had to say something about being "disappointed" in me. I hated that phrase because I did not want to let them down. They could also say simply, "You're acting like a child." I hated that even more. Perhaps, as an only child, I was driven to be more like the adults with whom I spent so much time. I even refused to eat the "child's plate" in restaurants. Obviously, "You're acting like a child" was a real insult.

I was taught by superb teachers, particularly in the fourth and fifth grades, where Mrs. Hagood and Mrs. Colquitt were able to convince me that I really was good at math. Mrs.

Hagood even played to our competitive instincts by seating in the front of the class those students who did best on the weekly test. This made me a lot more careful about avoiding errors because I really didn't like being in the back of the room.

My parents were very involved too. Like their friends, they were members of the PTA and attended the meetings. They checked my report card and discussed my progress with me at the end of each grading period. They were especially interested in my conduct grade. Disrespect for my teachers was simply not tolerated—my parents were, after all, teachers. But occasionally when they thought that I had been treated unfairly they took my side. One day the home economics instructor sent me home with a note saying that I was uncooperative. I had simply observed that the project of making bathroom curtains from towels with lace sewn on them seemed rather ridiculous. "You can buy curtains at Sears," I said, "and they look much better." My mother told the teacher that I had a point but insisted, nevertheless, that I make the curtains.

Though I did well, I have to admit that my study habits left something to be desired, given my strong tendency toward procrastination. Unfortunately, my parents, eager to help me succeed, probably reinforced this problematic instinct. One morning when I was in third grade, I woke up and realized that I'd forgotten to do a class assignment for that day. The task was to make a book with pictures that illustrated the story we were reading that week. Perhaps my parents should have just let me face the consequences. But they didn't. The three of us rushed around, cutting pictures from magazines, books, even the encyclopedia in order to finish the assignment. I got an A. All through school and college I was given to last-minute completion of my assignments and cramming for tests in all-night sessions. I'm afraid that procrastination remains a problem for me to this day. It's one of the few bad habits that my parents failed to cure me of when they had the chance.

I know this admission stands in contrast to the image that has emerged of me as a "grind"—someone who early in life studied all the time and did assignments well ahead of due dates. That description better fit my best friend, Velda Robinson, whom I adored but envied for her organized approach to her schoolwork.

The fact is, I was always more interested in other activities, such as piano. My parents were especially concerned that I did not love to read, as they did. They enrolled me in every book club known to man, but the books would just pile up unread. At one point they resorted to something called "Classic Comics," which were comic-book versions of works by authors such as Daniel Defoe and Mark Twain. I read principally when my schoolwork compelled me to do so. Eventually I discovered biography and found that I loved to read the stories of real—as opposed to fictional—lives. That is true to this day, though I still feel outmatched by the volume of books my friends and colleagues consume.

Despite my uneasy relationship with reading, my parents thought that I was a genius; they even arranged for me to take an IQ test at the age of six to prove it. When my score came back at 136—good but not Mensa level—they were convinced something was wrong with the test. But when I told them how hard I had found it to match the squares, circles, and stars with the correct hole in the puzzle, they calmed down. They hid whatever disappointment they might have felt at discovering that their daughter was, after all, a fairly normal little girl.

Yet there was no shortage of opportunities to develop the strengths that I did have and even some that I didn't. My Scouting career, for instance, was not wholly satisfactory. I was a Brownie and then a Girl Scout for a few years, and I was doing pretty well—until we got to the part about camping. One trip to the wilderness convinced me that I was not the outdoors type. In fact, the mosquitoes, heat, and warm Kool-Aid were enough to make me call my mother and tell her I wanted to go home. My parents picked me up, and to this day I've never tried camping again.

There were certain school activities I would have liked to do, but my parents quickly vetoed those ideas. When organizers of the school variety show cast me as one of the Supremes singing "Stop! In the Name of Love," my father decided that it would be undignified. Instead my parents hired Mrs. Clara Varner, the cosmetology teacher at Ullman, to teach me a tap-dancing routine to "Sweet Sue (Just You)" and "Sweet Georgia Brown." I was dressed in a blue leotard with tap shoes and a top hat, which my uncle had spray-painted gold. The routine was awful, but I gamely went out and performed. My father stood on the side of the stage, just in view of the audience, his arms folded sternly so no one would laugh. Given his imposing size, no one did. The end of my performance was greeted with applause. I was just glad it was over.

Outside of school, my parents provided me with a prodigious number of extracurricular opportunities. In addition to piano, I took all kinds of lessons: ballet, gymnastics, and even baton twirling, of all things. My mother decided that every well-bred young girl should speak French, so when I was eight my parents hired Mrs. Dannetta K. Thornton, who'd earned a master's degree in Romance languages and taught at Ullman, to give me French lessons on Saturdays. She transformed her basement into a French "salon" with all sorts of French pictures and artifacts. I liked Mrs. Thornton, but I didn't care much for the French language. Nonetheless, I kept plowing ahead and acquired enough of a foundation to continue my studies through high school and well into college. My parents also thought it important that I learn to type, just in case, and enrolled me in Saturday lessons with a teacher down the street.

I also played several sports. My friends contend that I was always a little lady in starched dresses, but I remember myself as bit of a tomboy who loved to tumble and run around. I ruined more than a few of those starched dresses, much to my mother's dismay and my father's delight. I also discovered that my parents' bed made a very nice trampoline.

Trying to cope with my excessive energy, my dad tried to interest me in organized sports and finally found one that I liked: bowling. He loved to bowl, and when Star Bowl opened in the early 1960s it became a regular stop for us on Saturdays. Usually Daddy would bowl with his friends from church and school early in the morning, and then there would be lessons and tournaments for the kids. Star Bowl kept its premises clean and had a recreation room that became a favored place to hold birthday parties and even an occasional wedding reception. In segregated Birmingham, gathering spaces were at a premium, so Star Bowl was a welcome addition.

I didn't, however, learn to swim. When I was six I swam a few times, but the next spring Mother said that there would be no lessons. In late 1961, Eugene "Bull" Connor, Birmingham's commissioner of public safety, had decided to close all recreational facilities rather than integrate them under court order. Not until I was twenty-five and living in California did I finally take swimming lessons. I suspect that there are a lot of black and white kids from Birmingham who learned to swim late in life thanks to Bull Connor.

The fact is, as hard as they tried, our parents could only partially succeed in building a fully adequate and parallel social structure. The time would always come when the children of Birmingham had to face the realities of segregation. For my friend Deborah Cheatham Carson it was when she asked if she could go to Kiddieland, an amusement park that her family passed on the way to her grandmother's house. Her father did not want to tell her that she couldn't go because she was black. So he said that Kiddieland wasn't good enough for her and that they were going to Disneyland instead. He then scraped together enough money to fulfill his promise.

One of my earliest exposures to segregation came when our family went to downtown Birmingham at Christmastime to see Santa Claus. Only about five years old, I overheard my father commenting that Santa seemed to be treating the black children differently from the white ones. My past encounters with Santa Claus hadn't been the best anyway— I'd taken one look at the big white man with a beard (likely the first one I had seen up close) and I slowly pulled away, eyeing him suspiciously. My parents had to intervene to get me to finish telling him what I wanted for Christmas.

But on this particular day, the Santa in question had been putting the white kids on his knee and holding the black children away from him, keeping them standing. "If he does that to Condoleezza," Daddy said to Mother, "I'm going to pull all of that stuff off him and expose him as just another cracker." I fearfully went forward, not knowing what to expect. Perhaps Santa felt the vibes from my father because he put me on his knee, listened to my list, and said, "Merry Christmas!" All's well that ends well. But I never forgot how racially charged that moment felt around, of all things, Santa Claus.

chapter thirteen

The only break from segregation came when we left Birmingham, which tended to be in the summer. When we would visit my grandmother and Aunt Theresa in Baton Rouge, we took the train, which provided integrated facilities.

We'd board the Silver Comet at about five in the evening in Birmingham, eat in the dining car, and sleep overnight in a bedroom berth. I can still taste the pudding, served in heavy silver ice cream cups, and feel the excitement of getting into bed as the train rushed along the tracks. But when we returned to Birmingham, the only place for blacks to eat out was A. G. Gaston's restaurant, and Mother didn't like to eat there because it was next door to a funeral home.

Once in a while we'd travel to Atlanta, about 150 miles away, where there was a wider variety of black restaurants and a nice movie theater. I can remember seeing Jerry Lewis's *The Nutty Professor* on one such occasion, being treated to dinner at Pasquale's, and then driving home since there was really no place to stay.

In 1959, my father decided to start graduate school. He wanted out of the ministry and into college work and began to pursue a master's degree in student personnel administration. The University of Alabama wasn't an option since it was segregated. As a result, many black professionals of my father's generation received their advanced degrees from midwestern or northern schools. Daddy learned that New York University had a fine program, and in the summer of 1959 and again in 1960, we packed up the family car and drove to New York City.

The problem was that there was nowhere for blacks to stay or eat until you reached Washington, D.C. The only option was a picnic lunch of fried chicken, pork chops, bread, and potato chips to eat in the car. Mother would get up very early and prepare the feast. We'd leave before daylight, hoping to make it out of the deepest South before dark. This was in the days before the interstate highway system was completed, and for a black family some of the roads in Georgia and South Carolina could be pretty scary.

When we reached Washington, D.C., we were all excited to be staying in a new chain of hotels called Holiday Inn. The rooms were hardly luxurious, but they were clean and it was a relief to have a bathroom. My parents, particularly my mother, were not too keen to stop at the gas-station restrooms for "coloreds" because they were almost always putrid and foul-smelling. If we couldn't find a reasonably clean bathroom when nature called, we just, shall I say, went in nature.

New York was fun. We ate at Howard Johnson's almost every night and went to the movies, including one that everyone was buzzing about, *Ben Hur.* We stayed in a nice hotel called the Manhattan until we started to run out of money. Then my father managed to get a small apartment in the quarters for medical students near Bellevue Hospital.

The second time in New York we began our stay in that complex. My mother didn't like the arrangements, though, complaining that the students would sometimes come home with blood on their clothes. I remember that there were quite a few roaches in residence too. Our dwindling resources and the less than ideal accommodations were taking a toll. Even I was able to tell that things were pretty tense between my parents. It was the first time I'd ever heard them yell at each other, and I was quite unnerved by the whole thing.

The next year my father decided to look for a more suitable place to pursue his studies. He learned that the University of Denver had a new program offering the degree that he wanted. More important, it offered reasonable student housing for families. So for the next two summers, when I was six and seven, we set out for a new destination: the Rocky Mountain state of Colorado.

The trip to Denver was longer than the trip to New York, but traveling westward, we were able to find lodging just across the Tennessee border. After a stopover we would resume driving, trying to make it as far as St. Louis or Kansas City, where we'd stop again. The car wasn't air-conditioned, and Kansas was always flat and hot. We would play all of those games that families do: How many different state license plates can you identify? Can you guess the number of miles to the next town? My parents developed another game: What colleges are located here? On one of these trips we actually went several hundred miles out of the way to see Ohio State. My parents counted the number of college campuses visited like some people count national parks.

But all in all I loved these trips. I'll never forget the first time we crossed the border into Colorado. When you reach Colorado, the horizon appears to rise and you know you're about to climb a mile high. My heart would beat faster as we drew closer to Denver, and to this day I am happiest in the high mountains of the western United States. I always felt that I should have been born in the West.

The move to Denver was a good one. The university had very nice accommodations for families in Aspen Hall, complete with a full kitchen. My mother was also able to enroll in classes. Her certifications to teach were in English and science, so, to capitalize on her music skills, she decided to pursue a third qualification in music.

The problem was what to do with me. There was a day camp to which I could and did go, but the activities ended in the early afternoon. One day we were passing by the campus ice arena, and I got an idea: ice-skating lessons. I'd seen two teenage figure skaters coming out of the arena in their little skating skirts. Since I loved watching figure skating on television, I was immediately taken with the idea. The Denver Figure Skating Club ran a full-day summer school at the University of Denver arena. Skating was therefore the perfect answer: an opportunity to learn something new *and* high-priced child care.

In short, the summers in Denver were ideal for the whole

family, with clean, cheap accommodations, educational opportunities for both Mother and Daddy, and skating for me. We discovered all kinds of activities in the relaxed atmosphere of Colorado. Evening trips to Elitch Gardens, an amusement park outside the city, were my favorite. I loved to ride the carousel and play the game where one throws balls at bowling pins, winning prizes for knocking them down. We went to see movies and discussed them afterward at a nice pizza parlor near the campus. When it was time to go home, I was really sad to leave and sorry to say goodbye to my new skating friends. Funny enough, I don't remember reflecting much on the fact that, for the first time in my life, my little friends were white.

chapter fourteen

When we returned home late in the summer of 1962, tensions were rising in Birmingham. Slowly but surely, the firewall separating the races was crumbling. Segregation was being challenged—and challenged hard—by the growing momentum of the civil rights movement, creating an atmosphere in Birmingham that was increasingly charged.

Over the years, officials in Birmingham had flagrantly ignored a series of landmark federal-level decisions. In 1957 Central High School in Little Rock, Arkansas, had been integrated with the help of federal forces. In Birmingham, however, *Brown v. Board of Education* had had little effect: the schools remained segregated. Similarly, the law requiring blacks to sit in the back of the bus had been declared unconstitutional after Rosa Parks raised national awareness with her refusal to give up her seat to a white man in 1955 in Montgomery. Still, Birmingham officials dragged their feet in desegregating the buses.

Several citizens' committees had tried to promote racial justice over the years. As far back as 1951, there had even been an Interracial Division of the Jefferson County Coordinating Council of Social Forces that was funded by the Birmingham Community Chest. But in 1956 the division was disbanded in the face of increasing hostility and violence. Several other efforts emerged during that period but quickly lost steam. When Alabama outlawed the NAACP that same year, the Reverend Fred Shuttlesworth formed the Alabama Christian Movement for Human Rights. Segregationists responded by bombing his house on Christmas night.

Throughout the late 1950s and early 1960s challenges to the system were met with growing violence. The singer Nat King Cole was attacked during his performance at Birmingham's Municipal Auditorium in 1956. In 1958 the Ku Klux Klan lit eighteen crosses throughout Jefferson County, and the next year they paraded through black neighborhoods. The Klan burned eleven schools the year after that.

There were decent people, many of them white, who were trying to do the right thing. In 1997, I was very proud to accept an honorary degree at the University of Alabama alongside Mrs. Virginia Durr, who, with her husband, had publicly challenged Bull Connor and other segregationists. The Russakoffs were among the many Jewish families who tried to cross color lines. And of course Judge Frank Johnson was a pioneering figure whose rulings started to bring change but also drew sharp criticism and put him and his family in danger.

In the face of these challenges, Birmingham's authorities remained steadfast in their insistence on segregation. Bull Connor became the fist of Jim Crow in the city and Governor George Wallace its soul in the statehouse in Montgomery. We watched on TV as Wallace stood in the doorway of the University of Alabama to prevent its integration. I'll never forget his infamous words during his inaugural address: "Segregation now, segregation tomorrow, segregation forever."

To be fair, around that time, my family had begun to experience small cracks in the walls separating the races. When I was about seven my mother developed a very bad bronchial infection. Nothing seemed to make her better. Desperate to find her proper care, my father asked Dr. Clay Sheffield, a white colleague, to recommend a physician.

And so on Saturday afternoon my parents and I went to visit Dr. Carmichael, an ear, nose, and throat specialist. We were escorted into the Negro waiting room, located up the back stairs above the pharmacy. The paint was peeling, the benches were pretty hard, and the wait was very long.

After Dr. Carmichael finally saw my mother, he called my father aside. "When you bring Angelena next week," he said, "come after five o'clock." The next Saturday we arrived after five o'clock and were escorted into the now empty white waiting room with large leather chairs and plenty of magazines to look at. Dr. Carmichael broke the rules because he respected my father as a human being. He was ready for change. Over time, the two waiting rooms merged and more black families joined us "up front."

I can remember, too, another act of "white kindness" that

occurred when at age seven I wanted desperately to go to the circus. Again, Dr. Sheffield came through, somehow wangling tickets. Unfortunately, I hated the circus and wanted to go home after a few minutes. My father, who'd moved heaven and earth to get the tickets, was furious. We stayed until the end.

Then there was the white saleslady who also found a way around the rules. One day Mother and I went to buy me an Easter dress. We were downtown at Burger-Phillips and a clerk whom Mother did not know said that I would have to try the dresses on in the storeroom. Blacks were not permitted in the fitting rooms. I remember it as if it were yesterday. Mother looked her dead in the eye. "Either she tries them on in the fitting room or we won't buy a dress here," she sternly replied. "Make your choice." The poor woman shooed us into the dressing room and stood guard outside, hoping that no one would see us.

But of course these breaks in segregation were isolated incidents. They were small cracks in the façade of a relentlessly unequal and demeaning system of racial separation. Parents in Birmingham made their children's opportunities as equal as possible and their worlds as pleasant as they could. Segregation did not intrude every day and people lived good lives. We found a way to live normally in highly abnormal circumstances. But there was no denying that Birmingham eclipsed every other big American city in the ugliness of its racism.

The history of the civil rights movement has been chronicled many times, and as a student of politics, I'm able to read these accounts with some measure of detachment. But I lived in Birmingham, and by 1962 my parents' attempts to shield me from the hostility of the place in which we lived were no longer succeeding. Birmingham would shortly become "Bombingham"; it was a very scary place.

chapter fifteen

It's funny what impresses you as a child. For me, the first salvo, the first shock of recognition, was learning of the boycott of the downtown stores in 1962. The action was organized to bring pressure on the stores to hire black clerks and to take down racial signage. That Easter everyone made sure to wear old clothes just to demonstrate that they were supporting the campaign.

But it was Christmas when I realized that something truly serious was under way. It had been our tradition to go downtown and see the elaborately decorated store windows at Pizitz and Loveman's. Much like Macy's in New York, the stores had animated mannequins in beautifully staged Christmas scenes. After viewing the windows, we'd always go into the stores and buy gifts for family, teachers, and friends.

But in 1962, my parents explained that we couldn't go to the stores because of something called a boycott. Black people were standing up for what was right, and we would too. I was terribly disappointed but old enough to understand the larger issues at stake. Strangely, we did go to visit Santa that year, though we didn't buy anything in the store.

Clearly, the boycott was succeeding. Sales declined 11 percent that year, leading the city of Birmingham to threaten to cut off a surplus food program servicing about nineteen thousand poor black families if the boycott didn't stop. The churches, including Westminster, responded by conducting a food drive to make certain that those families wouldn't be hurt.

Though they supported the boycott, my parents didn't want me to go without toys that Christmas, so they arranged for Aunt Gee to bring them from her home in Norfolk, Virginia. Santa Claus, therefore, showed up as expected with a Charmin' Chatty doll that spoke multiple languages. Like the iconic Chatty Cathy, the doll spoke when you pulled the string in her back. You could insert records in the side of *this* doll, however, and she would speak French, Spanish, and German. I loved her and got an early lesson in the fun of being multilingual.

Then came the crucible year of 1963 with its escalating challenges and violence. Throughout the winter and early spring, voting rights actions, sit-ins, and large protests removed any sense of normalcy in the city. In March two black candidates competed for spots on the Birmingham city council, and one of them received so many votes that he forced his opponent into a runoff election. And in April Albert Boutwell won the mayor's race, handing a defeat to Bull Connor as the city switched to a mayoral form of government.

Connor refused to step down, and for almost two months Birmingham had two governments. I'd never heard my father speak about any other human being the way he spoke about Bull Connor. He was, according to my father, the personification of evil. I hated him too and remember him as really ugly with a scowling, wrinkled face. I recoiled every time I heard him talking on television about the "Negras" who needed to be separated from honest white folk.

That same month, the Southern Christian Leadership Conference (SCLC) launched demonstrations to end segregation. George Wallace sent a hundred state troopers into Birmingham to reinforce the police. And on April 12, Good Friday, Martin Luther King Jr. was arrested in downtown Birmingham. From there he wrote his famous "Letter from Birmingham Jail."

In the midst of this turmoil, people had to make decisions about what role they would play. The epicenter of the civil rights movement became the black Baptist church, and the working classes served as its foot soldiers. The Reverend Fred Shuttlesworth, who had led the local chapter of the NAACP and eventually served as president of the national SCLC, left for Cincinnati in 1961 but returned frequently to Birmingham during the tumultuous days of 1963. Reverend Shuttlesworth has not, to my mind, received his due in the stories of these turbulent years. People in Birmingham know that it was he who was the heart and soul of the civil rights movement. The great national leaders Martin Luther King and Ralph Abernathy built on what Fred Shuttlesworth began.

My father and Reverend Shuttlesworth would sit on the

front porch at our house and talk late into the evening. I can remember bouncing over to them and climbing on Daddy's lap. He would shoo me off since they were often deep in conversation. We visited Reverend Shuttlesworth in Cincinnati in 1972, and the two men again spent long hours revisiting old times.

Nevertheless, I had always wondered if Reverend Shuttlesworth harbored any resentment toward my father for refusing to march with him. He has said that he thought that my father would not march because he feared his church would be bombed. While that doesn't really sound like Daddy, perhaps concern for his parishioners was indeed a consideration. And Reverend Shuttlesworth has always said that he knew that Reverend Rice was "there for him."

I gained a deeper appreciation for the respect the two men had for each other during a recent visit with Reverend Shuttlesworth, who, due to a stroke, can barely speak. He nodded when his wife asked if he remembered my father. "Were you good friends?" she asked. He nodded again. Then, when I handed him a picture of my father, he smiled broadly and kept running his hand across my father's face. "Oh, Condoleezza," he said. I cried because it spoke volumes about how he felt about my dad. They might have disagreed about tactics, but they cared for each other as friends.

Today there is a narrative that the middle classes who would eventually benefit disproportionately from desegregation did little to actually bring it about. It is true that few adults in my community marched with Martin Luther King. But the story of the choices that people made is far more complex than the caricature that neatly separates those who marched from those who didn't.

First, if you were black in Birmingham in 1963, there was no escaping the violence and no place to hide. What I remember most from this time is the sound of bombs going off in neighborhoods, including our own. Clearly, leaders of the movement such as attorney Arthur Shores were singled out. His home was bombed twice in 1963 and his neighborhood became known as "Dynamite Hill." But the white "night riders" and the KKK cared little about the role you played in the struggle; they were content to terrify any black family they could.

I can remember coming home from my grandparents' one night. We'd just gotten out of the car when we heard a loud blast down the street. In Birmingham that spring, no one had to think twice: a bomb had exploded in the neighborhood. In fact, it had been a gas bomb, hurled into the window of a house about a block or so away. My father hurried my mother and me back into the car and started to drive off. Mother asked where he was going. "To the police," he said.

"Are you crazy?" she asked. "They probably set off the thing in the first place." Daddy didn't say anything but drove to the Rays' house in Hooper City instead.

Several hours later we returned home and learned that a second bomb had gone off. As terrorists still do today, bombers exploded the first device in hopes that a crowd would gather. They detonated the second bomb—filled with shrapnel and nails—in order to injure as many innocent onlookers as possible. Fortunately, people knew better, and no one went out into the streets after the first explosion. Still, no one slept that night. When we got home, Daddy didn't say anything more about the bomb. He just went outside and sat on the porch with his gun on his lap. He sat there all night looking for white night riders.

Eventually Daddy and the men of the neighborhood formed a watch. They would take shifts at the head of the two entrances to our streets. There was a formal schedule, and Daddy would move among the watchers to pray with them and keep their spirits up. Occasionally they would fire a gun into the air to scare off intruders, but they never actually shot anyone. Really light-skinned blacks were told to identify themselves loudly upon approach to the neighborhoods so that there wouldn't be any "accidents."

Because of this experience, I'm a fierce defender of the Second Amendment and the right to bear arms. Had my father and his neighbors registered their weapons, Bull Connor surely would have confiscated them or worse. The Constitution speaks of the right to a well-regulated militia. The inspiration for this was the Founding Fathers' fear of the government. They insisted that citizens had the right to protect themselves when the authorities would not and, if necessary, resist the authorities themselves. What better example of responsible gun ownership is there than what the men of my neighborhood did in response to the KKK and Bull Connor?

A second point worth making about the Birmingham movement was that Dr. King's strategy was hardly uncontroversial. Daddy sometimes derided those who later said they'd marched even though many had not. "If everyone who says he marched with King actually did," he once told me, "there wouldn't have been any room on the streets of Birmingham."

My father had his own reasons for refusing to join King in his acts of civil disobedience. I can remember as if it were yesterday a conversation between my parents about how to react to the call to take to the streets and behave nonviolently. I stood in the hallway of our house, listening as my parents conferred in the living room. "Ann, I'm not going out there because if some redneck comes after me with a billy club or a dog, I'm going to try to kill him," he said. "Then they'll kill me, and my daughter will be an orphan."

Years later I asked my dad if I had heard him correctly. He wasn't defensive about his refusal to march with Dr. King; in fact, he told me definitively that he didn't believe in being nonviolent in the face of violence.

He also hated the use of children and teenagers in the march. Out of frustration with the slow response to the protests, Martin Luther King and the movement preachers called children into the streets on May 2 for what became known as the Children's Crusade. Some of my friends were involved. James Stewart, George Hunter III (called "Third"), Raymond Goolsby, and Ricky Hall, all students of my father, were told to go out first and distract the police. Others were to follow and get as close to city hall as they could before being stopped. As they approached city hall from Sixteenth Street Baptist Church, Bull Connor yelled over the bullhorn, "Do you have a permit?" When they said that they didn't, he sent police to arrest the kids. When the kids kept coming, he called in police dogs and turned fire hoses on the marchers. These young kids had been led straight into the teeth of Bull Connor's henchmen. The rightness of their cause aside, my father was appalled at what he saw as endangering innocent children.

Daddy nonetheless did what he could to support his students. On that day and several to follow, large numbers of high school students left school and joined the marchers. My father, their teachers, and for the most part their parents tried to dissuade them, saying they should fight racism with their minds, not their bodies. But when the Birmingham Board of Education demanded that the teachers report "absences" so that the kids could be disqualified for graduation, they refused. Students were encouraged to come to school, be marked present, and then leave for the protests. The teachers would turn their heads while the students left.

By the afternoon of May 2, policemen had arrested hundreds of students, and when the jails couldn't hold any more protesters, the police shipped them off to the fairgrounds. My father received permission to go and walk among the kids so that he could report to their parents that they were safe, and I went with him. After a couple of days of crowded conditions—so crowded that the students had to sleep in shifts because there was no room to lie down—the adults had had enough. They mobilized lawyers to get the kids released.

The images of Bull Connor's dogs and fire hoses confronting unarmed, peaceful protesters in Kelly Ingram Park, located in downtown Birmingham directly across from Sixteenth Street Baptist Church, are some of the most indelible in American history. During that long, hot summer of 1963, Bull Connor even brought "irregulars" from the backwoods of Alabama to do the dirty work that even the police would not do. My folks and I would watch them streaming down Sixth Avenue in pickup trucks adorned with Confederate flags. Trying to intimidate us, they hung out of the windows and brandished sawed-off shotguns. The protesters met even these goons with dignity and reserve and refused to be provoked.

But on the night of Saturday, May 11, Bull Connor's militia met up with a different kind of black protester. A full-scale riot erupted after the Ku Klux Klan bombed the A. G. Gaston Motel in an attempt to assassinate Martin Luther King, who had left the city hours earlier. Black protesters threw bricks at officers and attacked police cars in the area around the motel. Another large group of young men had gone drinking at an establishment on Fourth Avenue. "Lit up," as Southerners put it, with various strains of alcohol, they joined in the riot and marched on Kelly Ingram Park. The marchers encountered an armored personnel carrier parked there, and rumors spread that Bull Connor was in it. The men set fire not only to the carrier but also to nearby patrol cars and pickup trucks. Members of the mob were arrested and hauled off to jail, but the "resistance" had an effect. My parents wanted me to feel safe, but they also wanted me to see what was going on. The next morning, we drove down to Kelly Ingram Park, where one could see the carnage of burned vehicles and quite a few irregulars heading for home.

Ironically, we should have been in Denver as these events unfolded. I've often wondered why my parents were so insistent on staying home in 1963. If ever there had been a time to go to Denver for as long as possible, this would have been

it. But we didn't and thus witnessed the violence and turmoil. When I later asked them why, they didn't really have
a good answer. After I pushed, my father finally said that he
had to be with his congregation. Perhaps it just seemed
wrong to abandon Birmingham in the midst of the struggle.

The summer of police dogs and fire hoses finally captured the
attention of the nation. Birmingham was clearly exposed as
a city of appalling hatred, prejudice, and violence. That hatred found full expression on September 15, 1963, when a
bomb at Sixteenth Street Baptist Church killed four little
girls who were on their way to Sunday school.

Services hadn't yet begun at Westminster that Sunday,
but the choir, elders, and ushers were already in the sanctuary. I was there with my mother as she warmed up on the
organ. All of a sudden there was a thud and a shudder. The
distance between the two churches is about two miles as
the crow flies, but it felt like the trouble was next door. After
what seemed like hours but was probably only a few minutes,
someone called the church to say that Sixteenth Street Baptist had been bombed. No one knew how many other
churches might have been targeted.

My father didn't try to conduct the service but somehow
thought it safer if people remained together in the church.
An hour or so later word came that the bomb had killed four
little girls who were in the bathroom. I don't remember how
long it was, but we soon knew their names: Denise McNair,
age eleven, and Addie Mae Collins, Cynthia Wesley, and
Carole Robertson, all age fourteen. Two other black children
would die that day in racially motivated attacks. Everyone

was scared and parents just wanted to get their children home.

Back at home we turned on the television. Footage from the bombed-out church was all over the news, along with the unbelievably sad pictures of little bodies being removed from the wreckage and taken away in hearses. My parents were constantly on the phone with members of the family and their friends across Birmingham. The men of the community took up the neighborhood watch. But I remember feeling that they were really powerless to stop this kind of tragedy. I just sat and watched television. When it came time to go to sleep, I asked if I could sleep in my parents' bed.

I stayed home from school the next day, as did all of my friends. My father and mother went to work, but I went to Grandmother's house. She was as dazed as anyone else and just kept saying that the Lord worked in mysterious ways. I remember thinking that these mysterious ways were awfully cruel, but I didn't say anything to my devout grandmother.

The outrage would settle on our community, but at first we were just sad. Birmingham isn't that big, and everyone knew at least one of those little girls. This was a deeply personal tragedy. Cynthia and Denise were from the neighborhood. I knew Denise best; though she was older, we would still play with dolls together. Her father was our milkman and a part-time photographer who worked at everyone's birthday parties and weddings. Denise had been a student in my father's first kindergarten.

My uncle had been Addie Mae Collins' teacher, and he cried like a baby when he saw her picture on the news and again when he saw her empty chair the next day. Mr. John

Springer, one of my father's closest friends, lived next door to the McNair family. He had not left for church that morning. A while after the bomb went off he saw people running toward the McNairs' house. "I just heard Maxine wail," he told me later. "The door was closed, but she cried out so loud that I just knew what had happened."

Three of the girls were eulogized on the Wednesday after the bombing, and the other, Carole, on Tuesday at the Methodist church. We tried to go to the funeral for the three, at which Dr. King officiated, but by the time we arrived at the church it was filled to capacity, so we stood outside on the steps. Three of my father's students—fifteen-year-old James, Ricky, and Third—were pallbearers. Ricky almost collapsed, but James held him up. I don't remember much except the recessional of coffins. They were small and white. In my mind's eye, though, one of the coffins was pink.

The homegrown terrorism against Birmingham's children seemed finally to rock the nation's conscience. On June 11, President John F. Kennedy had delivered a historic address calling for an end to segregation and introduced a legislative package in Congress to do so. The proposed Civil Rights Act sought to atone for the systematic prejudice and oppression that characterized the South by banning segregation in public accommodations and allowing the federal government to join in state lawsuits to integrate public schools. Although this effort had begun months earlier, we believed the tumultuous summer of 1963—culminating in the horrific deaths of four little girls at the hands of violent extremists—would give the young president greater impetus to act.

I can remember my father, who hadn't voted for John

Kennedy, saying that he hoped the President had the muscle to carry through. If this attempt failed, he told my mother, the segregationists would be emboldened and life in Birmingham would be intolerable. He said that now that the hornets' nest had been stirred, white supremacy would either die or triumph completely. There was no middle ground.

We followed events in the nation's capital through the daily reporting of Chet Huntley and David Brinkley. For us this wasn't just some academic political debate; it was personal. We felt that our fate was completely in the hands of the Kennedys.

That Friday, November 22, 1963, started like any other. In the most remarkable way, life had become more normal again after the awful events two months before. I was in Mrs. Riles' geography class, which would be followed by recess and then history, which Mrs. Riles also taught. Suddenly one of the other teachers rushed in to tell her that the President had been shot in Dallas.

It was nearly time for recess anyway, so Mrs. Riles shooed us out onto the playground and headed to the teachers' lounge to watch the reporting. I stood around with my friends on what was a pretty warm day for late November, not really knowing what to do.

Eventually the bell rang. We went back into the classroom, and Mrs. Riles started to teach again. A few minutes later, she stopped and went to the door. I heard her wail. "The President's dead," she said, "and there's a Southerner in the White House. What's going to become of us now?"

School was dismissed, and I went to my uncle Alto's

classroom. We got in the car and headed to my grand-mother's house, as we always did. He turned to me and said, "How do you feel?"

"Do you mean about the President?" I said. He nodded, and I told him that I was very sad. "And scared," I added. Alto didn't ask why, but Mrs. Riles had given me a reason.

It's true that Americans of a certain age remember where they were when they heard that President Kennedy had been shot. That night's evening news and the constant replaying of the motorcade, the moment of impact, and the slumping President are images so vivid as to seem like yesterday. So too are the dignity of Jacqueline Kennedy, the swearing in of Lyndon Johnson, and the funeral cortege making its way mournfully through Washington, D.C. But for black citizens of Birmingham, John Kennedy's assassination was personally threatening. I doubt if many children outside the South would have described their reaction to his death as fear.

Fortunately, though Lyndon Johnson was a southerner, he carried through on Kennedy's promise to end segregation. As a political scientist, I have read scores of academic papers on Johnson's legislative approach. Some believe that Johnson was able to do what Kennedy could not have: assemble a coalition of northern Democrats and liberal Republicans to ram through landmark legislation. Donald Rumsfeld, then a young congressman from Chicago, was one of the Republicans who supported the President. I can dispassionately an-alyze Johnson's strategy and the shameful reaction of the Republican Party that resulted in the "Southern strategy," a conscious attempt to court white voters disgruntled by desegregation. But I have to step out of my own experience to do so because this was not just any legislation—it produced fundamental changes in my family's lives. And it did so almost immediately.

On a hot July day in 1964, we watched Huntley and Brinkley deliver the news that the Civil Rights Act of 1964 had passed the U.S. Congress and had been sent to the President for his signature. Johnson would sign the legislation on July 2. The local news anchor repeated the story after the national news. "The so-called Civil Rights Act passed today," he intoned, adding a rather telling qualifier to his description of the legislation.

But it didn't matter. A couple of days later, my father said, "Let's go out to dinner." We got dressed up and went to a relatively new hotel about ten minutes from our house. We walked in, and people literally looked up and stopped eating. But in a few minutes, perhaps recognizing that the law had changed, they went back to eating, and we were served without incident. A few days after that, however, we went to a drive-through hamburger stand called Jack's. It was nighttime, and as I bit into my hamburger, I told my parents that something tasted funny. Daddy turned on the car light. The bun was filled with onions: nothing else, just onions.

Nonetheless, de jure segregation was over. Decent people—not extremists, but ordinary people—would start to adapt to that fact. Much is rightly made of the historic significance of the Voting Rights Act of 1965. But in terms of daily life, the Civil Rights Act of 1964 was at least as important, striking down legal segregation.

Many years later when I was national security advisor I was shocked to learn that this wasn't universally understood.

One day in a meeting to plan the President's calendar, we reviewed a request to commemorate the fortieth anniversary of the Civil Rights Act. The consensus was that the President could issue a paper statement without much fanfare because the fortieth anniversary of the 1965 Voting Rights Act was to be celebrated the next year, and that legislation was considered to be the real breakthrough. I hit the roof and, more pointedly than perhaps I should have, told my colleagues that they'd better understand that the 1964 act was the one that had made it possible for me to eat in a restaurant in my hometown. Taken aback, they relented, and we had a very nice celebration in the East Room. We invited Lynda Bird Johnson Robb, whom I had the chance to thank personally for the courage and commitment her father had shown in bringing about dramatic changes in my life.

chapter sixteen

To be honest, some things remained the same after the 1964 legislation. The schools, for instance, remained segregated in all but name. Yet interaction between white and black students began to occur. In the fall of 1964, our school was selected to participate in the first integrated book fair, where students displayed books that they'd read along with a little synopsis of the story.

Mrs. Hattie Witt Bryant Green, who was the library teacher and very demanding, carefully prepared us for the big day at the Tutwiler Hotel. We weren't going to embarrass ourselves, she told us, in this first academic encounter with white people. Mrs. Green paid attention to every detail, insisting that the girls wear bows in their hair and that the boys wear ties. When we arrived at the hotel we found that we had been assigned to a separate room, but whites came through and looked at our projects, and we looked at theirs.

After the event, Mrs. Green proudly pointed out that she never would have allowed her students to display projects as shabby as the ones the white students had created.

There were new opportunities for my parents too. The black and white presbyteries (the regional governing bodies of the church) merged, and my mother's choir had an opportunity to sing at a white Presbyterian church. Daddy had tried to break down racial barriers much earlier and had befriended a number of white ministers. A few Sundays after the Civil Rights Act passed, he got an alarmed call from one of these pastors. "Reverend Rice," he said, "there are some Negro people out in front of the church and it seems they want to worship. What should I do?" My father replied that they probably weren't there to make trouble, just to worship, and that the best thing to do would be to greet them and seat them. His friend called after the service to say that all had gone well.

A few days later my father came home from school really excited to say that Dr. Sheffield wanted him and another guidance counselor, Mrs. Helen Heath, to be the first blacks to work for the state of Alabama at the employment office downtown. They would be trained at the University of South Carolina and spend the summer counseling in vocational education. He added that the clients and their fellow workers would be black *and* white. Mrs. Heath remembers that Dr. Sheffield also said that he wanted them to teach white people how to say "knee-grow." The time for saying "Negra" had long passed.

I was really disappointed that we would not be going to Denver for the summer, but the trip to Columbia, South

Carolina, was fun, especially since we got to fly on an airplane for the first time. I bought a new pink and white checked dress to wear aboard the Southern Airways flight.

That summer featured another highlight as well. I was almost ten and had begun to tire of the piano. Grandmother had stopped teaching, and Mother took up the role of my music instructor. This was not a good development. I can remember Mother yelling out from the kitchen as I practiced. "That's not right!" she'd call out.

"You're not supposed to be listening. I'm *practicing*," I would respond.

Somehow we just didn't have the right chemistry for this endeavor. I told my mother I wanted to quit. I can remember her response as if it were yesterday. "You are not old enough or good enough to make that decision," she said. "When you are, you can quit." I was shocked, but I could tell that there wasn't any room for debate.

Mother and Daddy decided that I needed a change to reinvigorate my interest. As it happened, Birmingham-Southern College had a very fine conservatory of music, but to date its student body had been exclusively white. My father called and said that he had a child who was an accomplished pianist and wanted to study at the conservatory. Several weeks passed, but I was granted an audition.

On the day of the audition I admitted to my parents that I was nervous. They were surprised because I had always displayed rock-solid nerves while performing in piano recitals or concerts. After all, I had been doing so most of my life. They asked if I needed more time to prepare. I finally admitted that I didn't want to embarrass anyone. I'd be the first black student in the Birmingham-Southern program. I felt that I was carrying the weight of needing to be twice as good. They reassured me that I was indeed twice as good. Looking back, it is striking that they didn't say, "You *don't have* to be twice as good."

The audition went very well, and I was admitted. I got back into the car completely elated. We went to Forbes Piano store to buy the prescribed curriculum, and I was soon reenergized in my pursuit of a career as a concert pianist. Years later, my father said that he was really glad that he and my mother took the chance of letting me try to break this color barrier. He then laughed. "They were probably just relieved that you didn't dance on the piano."

As desegregation continued to take hold, social life changed too. We went to restaurants frequently and were generally treated with respect. And we took in a movie once in a while and went twice to the traveling ice show Holiday on Ice.

Then, in 1965, the NFL played its first professional football game in Birmingham's newly desegregated Legion Field, pitting the Dallas Cowboys against the Minnesota Vikings. Even though my mother's father was gravely ill—he died the next day—Mother went to the game to keep from disappointing me. She knew I regarded it as a watershed event.

Mother and I bought new matching outfits: navy blue suits with gold blouses and gold hats. We sat in our seats and began to watch the game. Former Olympic gold medal sprinter Bob Hayes was a rookie wide receiver for the Cowboys, and he took the opening kickoff and ran it back ninety-plus yards. We cheered wildly. I don't think my parents knew that I heard the man behind us say, "Oooh-wee. Look at that nigger run!"

We stayed in Birmingham only one more year before moving to Tuscaloosa, where my father accepted a job as dean of students at Stillman College. Over the years, Birmingham has remained fixed in my mind as a place and an experience inextricably bound up with those troubled times. A great deal has changed, including the election of successive black mayors and city council members (not least my friend Carole Smitherman). Ironically, Bull Connor's successor many times removed was, until recently, a black woman.

The schools are completely integrated, and though neighborhoods are still largely segregated in the de facto sense, even that is breaking down. In the suburbs where we once shopped to purchase the higher-quality goods of white merchants, affluent blacks and whites, including my aunt Gee, live side by side.

When I visited Birmingham in 2003 my aunt Connie threw a party for me, inviting my friends from school and several teachers. Everyone was, of course, black. But the caterers were white. No one else seemed to notice. I asked Connie how she'd selected them. "The mother of one of my students started a catering service," she replied. "I thought I'd give her a chance." This was perfectly logical but out of bounds for the Birmingham that I had known and left as a child.

Back in 1961, CBS did a devastating documentary called *Who Speaks for Birmingham?* The film is filled with whites and blacks talking about life in "The Magic City," as Birmingham is called. Several white citizens explain why race mixing is against natural law and why the "Negras" are happy with the way things are. My parents and I watched it at the time and were appalled, angry, and hurt.

I once again saw clips of the documentary in 2005 when I took British Foreign Secretary Jack Straw and his wife, Alice, as well as British Ambassador David Manning and his wife, Catherine, to the Birmingham Civil Rights Institute. My father's longtime friend and colleague, Dr. Odessa Woolfolk, walked us through the exhibits that chronicled segregation. I was proud of what we had overcome, but as I noticed the horrified looks on the faces of my guests, I became deeply embarrassed. How could it be that so much hatred and prejudice had been lodged in one place? And how could it be that this was the place from which I had come?

In recent years I have been spending more time in the city with my family and friends, getting to know the "new Birmingham." Birmingham's efforts to emerge from the dark shadows of that time are now decades old. Yet I want to be a part of that emergence because somehow it is important for me to come to terms with and feel good about the city of my birth.

chapter seventeen

My father came home one day and he and my mother went into their bedroom, closed their door, and began talking. I couldn't hear the words, but it sounded like a very serious discussion. I wasn't used to being shut out of my parents' deliberations. We talked about everything—or at least I thought we did.

When they emerged my mother was crying. Daddy wanted to take a job as dean of students at Stillman College in Tuscaloosa, sixty miles from Birmingham. My mother, whose life had been spent in Birmingham and whose recently widowed mother was there, did *not* want to move. My parents had finally bought property, a plot of land adjoining one owned by my uncle Alto and his wife. They were planning to build there in a kind of family compound. Moreover, Mother was gaining more and more acclaim for her cultural productions at school and for the excellence of Westminster's choir. And, she told my father, "Tuscaloosa is in the boondocks."

I wasn't thrilled with the idea of moving either. What about my piano lessons at Birmingham-Southern? What about my friend Velda Robinson, whom I saw at school every day, and Margaret and Vanessa, with whom I played in the neighborhood every evening?

My father was unmoved. Daddy wanted desperately to get out of the pulpit and into college work and he was determined to take this opportunity. This was, for him, a logical extension of his commitment to youth in his ministry. So when Stillman called he felt it was time to go.

I was shocked to learn that he had already decided to accept the job before asking my opinion. I challenged him about it, saying that it was my life too. He actually apologized but said that it was time to leave Birmingham. We would come back every Wednesday so that I could continue my lessons at Birmingham-Southern. And I could call Velda every night if I wanted to.

Several days later we went down to visit Tuscaloosa. My mother was reassured when she was offered a job teaching at Druid High School. Daddy had been given a large house on Geneva Drive on the small, quiet campus. Pretty soon Mother set about having it redecorated, clearly impressed with the fact that it was much nicer than our little manse in Birmingham.

Life in Tuscaloosa was very different, largely because our lives revolved around the college. Stillman was a small college then, of about 650 students, but it had a very nice, well-appointed campus. For the first time, I could wander about unaccompanied because the campus was isolated and safe. I would often walk the quarter mile to the student union, where there was a bowling alley, or over to my father's office on the main quadrangle. My father even took advantage of the isolation of the campus to teach me at the age of eleven to drive along some of the back roads.

Stillman had no football team but an excellent basketball team, which we followed passionately. We occasionally went to see the University of Alabama play football and began to develop an affinity for the Crimson Tide, which survives with me to this day.

The University of Alabama, just a few miles from Stillman, also provided a whole new range of educational activities. My parents made certain that I spent a good deal of time on the newly integrated campus, attending the university's speakers series and touring science labs and the library. Sometimes after school we would just go up to the campus and walk around. The speakers series was particularly stimulating. We saw both Robert F. Kennedy and David Brinkley, our family's media hero, at the university's new field house.

When it came to my formal schooling, however, things were more complicated. In my last year in Birmingham, I'd been one of a few sixth graders who'd been merged into the seventh-grade classroom. We did our sixth-grade work but joined the seventh graders for their math, science, and reading curriculum. But when we moved to Tuscaloosa, there was no such program. Placing me in seventh grade would have meant repeating much of the curriculum. Yet skipping a grade meant that I'd be eleven in eighth grade until November and then only twelve.

My parents were worried because there is a huge difference between eleven-year-old girls and thirteen-year-old girls. Arguably, seventh grade was the worst possible one to skip. We discussed the issue as a family. It was the first time that I heard about something called puberty, my parents saying that I'd be behind my classmates in both physical and social development. I can remember sitting on the living room sofa, waiting patiently while my parents fumbled for the right words to explain what they meant. There were long pauses during which they'd look at each other. My father, who was one of the most articulate people I knew, was, for the first time in my experience, tongue-tied. He looked down and stopped trying. So Mother took up the task, delivering a rather opaque and disjointed lecture on sexuality. I was bemused, taking from her remarks something about needing to stay away from boys and their raging hormones, whatever those were. I didn't ask questions. I felt bad for my folks because they were so clearly embarrassed by the whole discussion. I didn't bother to tell them that I knew quite a bit about all of this from another source, my friends' older siblings. At the end I just said okay, and the conversation ended.

Ultimately, I decided to go to eighth grade. I could tell that my parents wanted me to, but they really didn't push. They didn't have to because it was an easy decision for me. I had always wanted to be one of the "big kids."

It turned out, though, that fitting in was not as easy as I had imagined. I had only recently stopped playing with Barbie dolls, and now all my friends wanted to talk about were their boyfriends. I experienced early puberty, but I was still underdeveloped compared to my classmates. Eventually, though, I adjusted. I found a new best friend in Donna Green, who, like me, loved watching *Dark Shadows* on television after school.

In fact, my parents were a bit concerned when I suddenly announced that I had a boyfriend too. His name was Darrell Bell and he was a drummer in the Druid High School band. My parents felt better when they learned that he was the son of the school guidance counselor. I guess they decided that with that parentage, Darrell couldn't get too far out of line.

I came to enjoy Druid and did well academically. I became less conscious of the age difference with my classmates. But for my mother, things were not working out as well. The school principal, Mr. Hughes, and my mother clashed repeatedly. When my mother was assigned one of the classroom annexes, actually a trailer, on the field next to the lunchroom, she took this as another affront, and she and the principal got into a loud argument. I recognized Mother's shrill voice immediately as she screamed at Mr. Hughes, "Don't you ever come into my classroom unannounced and complain about my teaching!"

Mr. Hughes almost ran out of the room, yelling as he left, "That Rice woman is crazy!"

The kids in the lunchroom were laughing uncontrollably. I laughed too. Maybe I should have been embarrassed, but I loved it when my mother stood up for herself, even if she made a bit of a spectacle in doing so.

Obviously, Mother's relationship with Mr. Hughes was irrevocably broken after that. The next year, Tuscaloosa was opening two new middle schools, Woodlawn and Tuscaloosa Middle School, and the pressure was growing to integrate the schools and particularly the teaching staff. As it happened, my mother was assigned to the white school, Tuscaloosa. She was excited to be going there, breaking the color barrier and teaching in a new environment. But before the school year started, she was reassigned to the black school, Woodlawn, without explanation. She was crestfallen, feeling that she'd been demoted. But she tried to make the best of it. She started a new arts program at Woodlawn and was put in charge of the opening ceremonies and cultural presentation for the school's inauguration. Still, working in a middle school was not nearly as fulfilling for her as teaching at Western-Olin had been.

Daddy's career was flourishing in Tuscaloosa, however. He was right that college work suited him. Easily the most popular figure on the Stillman campus, he was also one of the movers in the city of Tuscaloosa. He was asked to speak everywhere, and everyone from the mayor to the leadership of the University of Alabama consulted him. Daddy struck up a friendship with the vice chancellor of the university, a man named John Blackburn, who would figure heavily in Daddy's career advancement for years to come.

I remember how busy my father was in those days. Daddy was determined to take advantage of the numerous new "Great Society" programs sponsored by the federal government. He was the acting director and a counselor in the Upward Bound program at Stillman, less than a year after the Higher Education Act of 1965 created it. And Daddy's church had housed one of the first Head Start programs back in 1965, so now in Tuscaloosa he was asked to chair the advisory board of the program. I could tell that he was a very important man in the community and I was very proud of him.

Yet John W. Rice Jr. was never one to grow complacent, and Daddy decided that Stillman's students were hearing too little about the social and political events of the day. Daddy received permission from the new president, Harold Stinson, to start a speakers series. Dr. Stinson was shocked when he learned that Daddy had invited as the first speaker Stokely Carmichael, the firebrand radical leader of the Student Nonviolent Coordinating Committee (SNCC).

Alabama had just begun to settle down from the upheavals of the past years. Not surprisingly, the thought of having Stokely Carmichael in Tuscaloosa was jarring. Stokely belonged to the new breed of radical black leaders. It was a time when the Black Panthers were a real and violent force on the West Coast and Malcolm X and the Nation of Islam were coming into their own. Stokely was making waves with incendiary language about the Vietnam War and white America. These were not people in the mold of Martin Luther King Jr., who believed in integration and the U.S. Constitution. They spoke in terms of revolution and blood, not in the language of nonviolence and civil disobedience.

A couple of days before Stokely was to speak in the Stillman College gymnasium, the Tuscaloosa chief of police called my father and asked to see him. "Reverend," he said, "Tuscaloosa just isn't ready for Stokely Carmichael. What if he starts some kind of riot? I don't want to stir up the rednecks either." Daddy reassured him. He'd talked with Mr. Carmichael, who wanted only to be heard. It would be good for the students, and any University of Alabama students who wanted to come were welcome too. After Stillman agreed to some extra security arrangements, the chief of police decided to let the lecture go forward. "Reverend Rice," he said, "I sure hope you know what you're doing." When he came home, Daddy told my mother and me that he'd assured the chief that he did indeed know what he was doing. Then he said, "I sure hope I do."

On the night of Stokely's appearance, the gymnasium was filled to capacity. Students *had* come from the University of Alabama, but none were white. Stokely, dressed in green fatigues, gave a stirring critique of American policy in Vietnam, adroitly displaying his rhetorical skills. The speech was radical. At one point he said that he had told the draft board to go ahead and draft him. "But don't expect me to use the gun on Vietnamese," he told the audience, implying but not saying that he might shoot American soldiers instead. "They classified me 4-F," he said, making reference to the draft category that meant "unfit to serve."

At the end, the place erupted in applause. We went backstage to see Carmichael. He was calm and courteous and told my father that Stillman College had been the first historically black college that had asked him to speak. Daddy replied that he believed in letting people speak, and he invited Stokely to come back the next year. It was the beginning of what would become a long and unusual friendship.

chapter eighteen

After settling in at Stillman, my father wanted to continue his graduate work. So in the summer of 1967 we resumed the practice of going to Denver as soon as school in Alabama was out of session.

Travel was much easier since hotels were now integrated all along the burgeoning interstate highway system. I was older and family games were replaced with Motown grooves and the latest rock anthems on the radio. My parents didn't complain, though they seemed slightly hurt when I indicated more interest in listening to the Temptations and Cream than in guessing the mileage to the next city or what college was located in that town.

The University of Denver had built new and quite pleasant graduate student housing. Mother resumed her music classes, and I returned to the ice-skating rink full-time, rising at four-thirty in the morning to make the first session at five.

I'd taken something of a hiatus from skating during our time in Denver in 1965, attending music classes with Mother. Now, in 1967, I dove into skating with renewed passion, spending the entire day at the rink and beginning to prepare seriously for tests and competition. The skating school was populated by very serious skaters, including a few destined for the Olympics. This time, when it was time to leave Denver, I really didn't want to go home.

When we returned to Tuscaloosa, I continued to progress both in social maturity and in the classroom. Life was good at Druid. But I longed to skate and Alabama had no ice-skating rinks. So I'd practice jumping on the floor in the den to the music of Schubert's Unfinished Symphony or Dvorak's *New World*. I made up routines that I looked forward to perfecting on the actual ice when we returned to Denver. As the summer approached, I grew more and more excited.

One afternoon in April, Mother and I had just returned from the home of the seamstress who was making a whole new skating wardrobe for me. As we walked into the house, we heard the news: Martin Luther King had been shot and killed in Memphis. My father came home immediately and we sat in the little den watching the assassination images play over and over on the television. No one could really believe it. My father had had his doubts about the strategy that King pursued in 1963, but he lionized King the man, like practically every other black person in America. I was sad. And I was angry.

The next day we went to school. I'd become a member of the Druid High School debate team and we were scheduled to go to Montgomery for the competition two days later. Our debate coach, who was the only white teacher at Druid (there were still no white students), called the team together and told us that we'd make the trip despite Dr. King's death.

For the first time in my life I had a strong political and racial reaction. How dare she be so clueless! My teammates and I asked her to leave the room and we held a meeting. We would refuse to go to Montgomery in honor of Dr. King. When the poor woman came back into the room she must have immediately sensed the hostility. She announced that participation in the meet would be voluntary. Of course, no one volunteered.

There was no school the day of the funeral. Again we watched television as a family, taking in the images of the fully veiled Coretta Scott King and the tiny King children. I cannot listen to "Precious Lord" to this day without a flood of emotion harkening back to that event:

> *Precious Lord, take my hand.*
> *Lead me on, let me stand.*
> *I am tired, I am weak, I am worn.*
> *Through the storm, through the night,*
> *Lead me on to the light.*
> *Take my hand, precious Lord, lead me home.*

Though I was only thirteen, 1968 was the year of my political awakening. It was one of those years that seemed to change things forever. It was not just the assassination of Dr. King. There was the Tet Offensive and the horrible pictures of Vietnam that suddenly filled our living room every night. I started to care what happened in Vietnam and would anxiously await Chet Huntley and David Brinkley's analysis. Then there were the May riots in Paris that introduced me for the first time to student radicalism. And on June 4, there was the news from Los Angeles.

My father was a political junkie, and we always watched election coverage. So there we were, glued to the TV set on the night of the California presidential primary in 1968, which would likely decide the Democratic nominee.

My father was a Republican, but this time he was going to cross party lines and vote for Bobby Kennedy. We all loved the Kennedys, Bobby most of all. He was, according to my father, ruthless in the pursuit of justice as attorney general and destined to be a great president. He just needed this victory in Los Angeles to defeat the "Happy Warrior," Hubert Humphrey, whom my father thought to be well-meaning but hapless.

The contest was very close and I was tired. As soon as Kennedy was declared the winner I went to bed, deciding to skip his acceptance speech. I'd just gone to sleep when my mother shook me and said, "Get up. Bobby Kennedy has been shot!"

My family gathered mournfully in the den. I sat on the carpeted floor, very close to the television set. We watched the footage of Bobby Kennedy lying on the floor, the huge football player Rosey Grier standing over him. We waited and waited. And then we heard. He was dead.

I had been sad and angry when Martin Luther King was shot. Now I was just devastated. What was happening to our country? That year would get worse. In August 1968, the

Soviet Union invaded Czechoslovakia, thousands of miles away from Birmingham. But I watched that too in horror. I felt terrible for Czechoslovakia's leader, Alexander Dubcek, and angry at the Soviet Union. My parents and I also watched the Democratic National Convention in Chicago, with the whole controversy about the seating of the alternative delegation from Mississippi and the brutality of the police against the demonstrators in the streets. Nineteen sixty-eight was a tough year to come of age politically. I was too young to do anything about what was happening but old enough to know that the situation was very bad. There had been a *Time* cover in 1966 that asked, "Is God Dead?" I hadn't dared ask my parents about it then, but in 1968 the question seemed inescapable.

One night, not long after the Chicago convention, I went to my father's study, sat down with him, and asked what he thought of what was occurring. I told him that I felt like there was chaos all around us and I was scared. His response was, in retrospect, not surprising given his conservative, religious perspective. He said that the values of the country had gone off track. People didn't respect each other, the country, God, or anything else anymore. But America was going to survive, he told me, even though it might not appear that way right now. He was devastatingly critical of Lyndon Johnson, even though he admired him for his role in the passage of the civil rights legislation, and also disapproved of Hubert Humphrey. Daddy told me he would vote for Richard Nixon, who would bring order.

* * *

Despite all the upheaval, we did make it to Denver in that summer of 1968. When we arrived, I went immediately to the ice rink, not even waiting to unpack. The schedule on the board showed me taking seven lessons each week, preparing for the battery of tests that rank skaters according to national standards. This was momentous news. I was going to train in the elite program that prepared skaters for competition.

My parents were very proud but told me that they couldn't afford seven lessons. They went to speak with one of my coaches, leaving me outside, and I assumed that they were explaining that they just didn't have the money for a full program. But after a little while, they emerged. I'd have the seven lessons a week as prescribed. I was thrilled and resolved to work very hard. I have no idea where or how they found the money. It wasn't the last time that they would exhibit incredible selflessness where I was concerned—nor was it the last time I would take their sacrifice for granted.

That summer I became really serious about my skating, and I got better fast. The problem was that we would soon return to Alabama, and one could only get so good practicing on the floor in the den. I couldn't believe my good fortune when my father asked me to call a family meeting: the subject would be whether to live in Denver for a full year.

My father had decided that he was never going to complete his graduate studies by taking two classes each summer. He had asked Stillman for a one-year leave of absence. Although he had been at the college for only two years, his request was granted. We would return to Alabama at the end of the summer, pack up what we needed, and return to Denver for the 1968–69 school year.

This all sounded great. But where would I go to school? And what about piano? I was doing very well at Birmingham-Southern. As it turned out, finding a piano program was easy. I would enroll at the University of Denver's pedagogical academy at the Lamont School of Music. The teacher gave me a full curriculum to study until I returned from Alabama.

The decision concerning my school was much harder. My parents weren't impressed with the Denver public school curriculum, which was at the leading edge of "experimental" education (read "not very structured or systematic"). Students were encouraged to be creative, even if they were wrong. "New math" was all the rage. My parents liked "old math" and thought that creativity was important, but only after you knew the basics.

They learned, however, that there was a really fine college preparatory program at George Washington High School that was very rigorous. They tried to get me admitted there. But it was not in the neighborhood in which we would be living (on the university campus) and I was denied entry. In fact, they were told that there was a chance that I would be sent to Manual High School, located in what could only charitably be called "the hood," because Denver had begun a busing program to achieve racial integration. My parents found this idea preposterous. They questioned the notion that black kids would learn better just by sitting in a classroom with white ones. This perhaps reflected their experience with excellent but segregated schools in Birmingham.

Now they were facing an almost laughable irony: their middle-class daughter could be bused across town to a poor black neighborhood in order to achieve desegregation. My parents decided to look for a private school alternative.

There were two possibilities: Kent Country Day School and St. Mary's Academy. Both were all-girls schools. My parents were more attracted to Kent initially, although it was more expensive. But on further examination, it became clear that St. Mary's, one of the oldest educational institutions in Denver, had a really outstanding college preparatory curriculum.

We visited St. Mary's, and I liked the campus and was excited at the thought of enrolling there. I filled out the application and was accepted before we left for Alabama. We also went to the Denver, the large department store downtown, and bought my new uniforms: a navy and green watch plaid skirt; white blouses; blue, green, and white sweaters; a green blazer for special occasions such as assembly; green, blue, and white knee socks; and saddle shoes!

With everything in place, we prepared to return to Alabama to execute the move west. Daddy had agreed to get the school year started at Stillman, so we would not return to Denver until October. I'd start school a month or so late, studying the St. Mary's curriculum at home in Tuscaloosa and trying not to fall behind.

My parents were very anxious to get home to Alabama because there was a lot to do. This resulted in one of my few real disappointments with them. I was scheduled to take a skating test on the Saturday morning that we were to leave. It would have necessitated a delay in our departure of about two hours. My father was adamant that we couldn't afford to wait and told me I could take the test when we returned in the fall. To this day, I still don't understand that decision. But grumpily I got in the car that morning and we set off for Alabama to prepare the move to Denver for one year. I secretly hoped that we'd never again live in Alabama.

My new life in Denver was very structured. Every morning I got up at four-thirty and headed to the rink at five. At seven I finished skating and went to school. After school I practiced piano, did my homework, and went back to the rink for another hour. Then I came back home and was in bed by nine-thirty. I had no free time and I didn't care. I loved the rigorous skating program, and my new piano teacher challenged me, insisting that I begin to participate in piano competitions. I could tell that I was advancing more rapidly than I had at Birmingham-Southern.

St. Mary's was a good fit for me academically. Though I was several weeks late in starting, I quickly caught up and had little trouble with the work. Socially, though, I hated the school. I didn't make friends very easily, unlike at Druid, where I had been popular. I'd gone from Alabama, where I never had a white classmate, to St. Mary's, where there were only three black girls in my entire class of seventy. Yet there seemed to be a huge wall separating me from my black sisters. Maybe I was just the new kid on the block, or maybe I didn't try hard enough, but I sure didn't feel welcomed by the few black students.

In general, I didn't care much for the social dynamics of an all-girls school. Life seemed to revolve around trying to attract the boys at our brother schools, Mullen Prep and Regis High. I explored becoming a cheerleader (one way to meet football players) but soon learned that the schedule interfered with skating. The only sport that St. Mary's played was field hockey, and after being hit with a stick during tryouts, I decided that the ice was friendlier. Most girls skied, a sport that I had neither the money nor, at the time, the inclination to try, fearing an injury that would end my skating season. St. Mary's didn't have a band, so that was out as an activity. I finally joined the glee club and was installed as the accompanist. I didn't love that either since I ended up playing for high-school sopranos who sang "Climb Ev'ry Mountain" from *The Sound of Music* with equal measures of gusto and horrendous pitch.

My parents certainly sensed that St. Mary's was not a perfect fit. They asked repeatedly whether everything was going okay. But that year I never confided my true feelings about the school. My parents were, after all, paying more than a thousand dollars in tuition—money they really didn't have. I wanted them to think that I liked St. Mary's and not worry. Moreover, it was just for a year, and my life revolved around skating in any case. I had plenty of friends at the rink, especially Debbie Mitchell, who was my closest buddy.

Debbie and I would skate every day and hang out together on the weekend. While we practiced, our fathers would stand and talk in the parking lot and got to know each other well. Debbie's father was Maurice Mitchell, the chancellor of the University of Denver. When my father finished his coursework that spring, Chancellor Mitchell offered him a job at the university.

Again we had a family meeting. I thought moving to Denver was a no-brainer. Though settling there would put my mother more than thirteen hundred miles from her mother, she too wanted to move and seemed confident that she could land a good teaching job. My father was a little worried because the financial package at the university wasn't quite as good as Stillman's. But after he worked out an arrangement for low-cost faculty housing, everything fell into place. My father returned to Alabama before the school year ended and resigned from Stillman. Mother and I followed as soon as school was out at St. Mary's. My dream had come true. We were going to live in Denver. Permanently!

chapter nineteen

We moved into one of the modest three-bedroom homes that were rented to young faculty at a highly subsidized rate for a maximum of two years. My parents gave me the master bedroom because it had its own bathroom and I was getting to the age where that kind of thing mattered.

One of our neighbors was an Israeli family. Benzion Netanyahu, a professor of Hebraic studies, taught in the Department of Religion, giving him and my father common interests. The Netanyahus had three sons, but only one was young enough to live at home. Their oldest son, Bibi, was in college, and their middle son was serving in the Israeli Defense Forces. Our families shared what I now understand to have been a Seder meal during the Passover holiday. Many years later, when Bibi Netanyahu was elected prime minister of Israel for the first time, my father reminded me of this example of far less than six degrees of separation. I still send greetings to Professor Netanyahu when I see his son.

Daddy started his job as assistant director for admissions and assistant dean of arts and sciences. Perhaps not coincidentally, his friend and mentor from Tuscaloosa, John Blackburn, had also moved to the University of Denver as vice chancellor.

It didn't take long for Daddy to become a major figure at the university even though DU could not have been more different from Stillman. Denver University was private and very expensive. It was known as a bit of a party school populated by rich kids who either couldn't get into Ivy League universities or wanted to ski—or both. Denver itself was more homogenous than almost any other big city in the country. I remember noticing that it was possible to spend an entire day on the city streets and not see another black person.

One of Daddy's responsibilities was to increase the diversity of the student body, and he was given wide berth to do so. He traveled extensively to major cities, recruiting black students to the university, which wasn't always easy. The mountain West could seem a bit foreign to kids who had grown up in places such as New York and Chicago. "The university should commit itself to the proposition that it is possible to have varying entrance standards, but only one exit or graduation standard," he argued, speaking to the heart of the affirmative action debate.

After one year, my father increased the number of black students at DU to about one hundred in a population of seven thousand. The key, he believed, was adequate financial support. "What good does it do to locate a student, get him or her to apply for admission, and then have no funds available?" he asked. In search of a sustainable solution, Daddy created the Education Opportunity Program, which administered grants to students who were receiving financial aid but needed additional help covering basic college expenses, such as books and rent. The program was unique, not because of its intent but because of the funding source: parking meters on campus.

But simply diversifying the student body was not enough. Daddy went to Chancellor Mitchell and Dr. Blackburn and told them that he wanted to develop a curriculum that would ensure that all Denver students fully understood black America. Daddy was keenly aware that Denver, as a private school, had considerable latitude in developing a curriculum of the kind he envisioned. In addition to a course that he taught on the history of Africa until 1800, he wanted to offer a seminar as a way of launching an effort to create more minority courses and appoint black professors in regular departments. "It's incomprehensible that out of all of the schools at DU you have one Afro-American administrator and two part-time people on the Faculty of Arts and Sciences," he noted. Daddy hoped the seminar was just the beginning, and with its broad conception, the seminar encouraged students to combine academic coursework with public service and community involvement.

The seminar was set to launch in the winter quarter of 1970. Daddy got into the car one day, almost giddy about the advertising flyers that he had just had printed. The flyers showed an American flag—with black stars and red and black stripes. "This will make them a little angry," he said. "That's good for this place."

The parade of speakers my father assembled for his seminar was extraordinary by any measure. Academics and educators, artists and activists, politicians and athletes all came together to provide their perspectives on the state of black America. There were also some civil rights leaders, such as Julian Bond, one of the founding members of the Student Nonviolent Coordinating Committee, and Fannie Lou Hamer, the woman who led the fight to seat an alternative delegation from Mississippi at the Democratic National Convention of 1968.

Sometimes the course resulted in direct action. For instance, during her speech to the class in 1970, Hamer mentioned that she had been unable to get federal examiners into Sunflower County, Mississippi, to ensure fair voting practices. Chancellor Mitchell, a member of the U.S. Commission on Civil Rights, took up the matter with the Department of Justice, which finally sent federal examiners to Mississippi. Hamer's lecture also inspired a large service project that included a citywide clothing drive on "Sunflower County Day," championed by Spencer Haywood and Larry Jones of the NBA's Denver Rockets. The entire Civil Rights Commission, headed by Father Theodore Hesburgh, the president of the University of Notre Dame, came for a class session the next year.

Occasionally, cultural figures such as the Ramsey Lewis Trio or the poet Useni Eugene Perkins were invited to perform. But most came from political backgrounds. A young

Charlie Rangel, then a state representative in the New York Assembly, joined Ralph Metcalfe, U.S. congressman from Illinois and founder of the Congressional Black Caucus, in the lineup.

And many of the speakers were on the radical end of black politics, such as Dick Gregory and Louis Farrakhan. Lou House and Charles Hurst came down from Malcolm X College in Chicago, and the three track stars made famous by raising their black-gloved fists at the 1968 Olympics—Tommie Smith, John Carlos, and Lee Evans—also spoke. One course session consisted of a telephone hookup to the hunger-striking black inmates of Attica prison in 1971. And, of course, Daddy invited his friend Stokely Carmichael to the podium several times.

The seminar had a pretty hard edge. This led my father, in a progress report on the class, to remind his unnamed critics in the university that the "deepest aims and hopes of the seminar are directed to the idea of reformation rather than revolution." "The seminar is *not* a staging ground for violent revolution," he emphasized. Daddy's point was that if the seminar encouraged greater demands from the black community, it should not be discounted as academically invalid.

In truth, my father was fascinated with the radical side of black politics. I was never taught that Farrakhan was a traitor or that the Black Panthers were terrorists. They were to be taken seriously on their merits. Years later, when so much attention was paid to then-Senator Obama's radical associations, I wondered what might have been made of the people who sat at our dinner table.

This was especially true of Stokely Carmichael, who came to Denver almost every year. Daddy even invited him in 1973 to speak at an adult education forum at the virtually all-white and quite wealthy Montview Boulevard Presbyterian Church, which we attended and where Daddy acted as a part-time assistant pastor. At the end of the session, Stokely, no longer in fatigues and now wearing tailored suits, received a standing ovation from the decidedly conservative membership. Afterward, my family and I were standing next to Stokely when we overheard a lady say, "Well, he wasn't so bad." Stokely turned to us without missing a beat: "What did she think I was going to do? Swing from the chandelier?"

Our association with Stokely Carmichael had an impact on me as well. When visiting the house he referred to me affectionately as his *"petite soeur,"* little sister. I remember sitting with him in the back seat of the car, singing along with the radio and witnessing his distress at lyrics that demeaned the black family. He hated the Temptations' "Papa was a rolling stone—wherever he laid his hat was his home." "Why do they send those messages to our kids?" Stokely asked.

Then, as I got older and my interest in Soviet politics grew, the two of us would debate his growing fascination with Leninism and socialism. He clearly thought that I was misguided in my rejection of communism and the teachings of Karl Marx. But Stokely Carmichael was a brilliant man and he made me hone my arguments. My father would beam as we argued, as he always enjoyed intellectual sparring and relished opportunities to "stir the pot."

Over the years I've reflected on what attracted my conservative, Republican father to radicals such as Stokely Carmichael. When I asked, he said that he liked the contestation of ideas. It's true that he loved to make people uncomfortable by testing the limits of their intellectual tolerance—whether with his congregation in Bible study or his students in the classroom.

But I've come to believe that there was more to it. Daddy would sometimes ridicule those who suggested that blacks find succor and support in a closer association with Africa. "America is our home," he'd say. "Africa doesn't belong to us or us to it." And he'd sometimes say to my horror that the tragedy of slavery had given us the chance to live in the freest and most prosperous country on earth. He loved the United States of America and was vocal in his appreciation for the good fortune of being American. Yet he clearly admired the willingness of radicals to confront America's racism with strength and pride rather than with humbleness and supplication.

Daddy was remarkably adept at navigating and charting a course for success in the white man's world. But there was, I know, a deep reservoir of anger in him regarding the circumstances of being a black man in America. On occasion it surfaced—for instance, when Santa Claus was about to mistreat his daughter. Sometimes, after integration took hold, he and my uncle Alto would laugh at the "shuffling" white service people who were grateful for a tip from them. "He ought to scrape and bow for how he treated my daddy," I overheard Alto say one day. My father roared his approval. But for the most part my father couldn't afford to let the bitterness interfere or to give expression to it. Maybe giving voice to black radicals in the midst of his very white world helped him to square the circle.

So just one year into his tenure at Denver, Daddy's career was flourishing, and his class was drawing crowds. I too was doing considerably better at St. Mary's, making new friends there. I won the state championship in Greek and Roman history, finding a new passion. Well, actually it was only a competition among parochial schools, so there weren't that many contestants. Nonetheless, my parents were very proud.

There *was* one unpleasant incident at St. Mary's, which did cause my parents to question their decision to send me there. After doing poorly on the Preliminary Scholastic Aptitude Test (I wasn't then and am not now good at standardized tests), the guidance counselor called me in to review the results. "You didn't do very well," she said, ignoring the fact that I was two years younger than my schoolmates. "Perhaps you should consider junior college." I just laughed at her, thanked her for her advice, and left. But when I went home and told my parents, they were *not* amused. They wanted to go to the school and confront her. I begged them not to, and I prevailed. I have told that story many times since, particularly when I was provost at Stanford, for several reasons. First, my own experience has led me to be rather suspicious of the predictive power of standardized tests. Second, I realize how lucky I was that my own sense of self—developed through years of parental affirmation—shielded me at that moment from self-doubt. I have always worried that there are many young people, particularly minorities, who might internalize negative messages like that and simply give up.

On balance, though, I loved my life in Denver. I kept the same rigorous schedule of piano and skating that I'd established the year before. I made rapid progress in piano in particular, competing in statewide and regional competitions. My first major competition was something of a disaster, though. Playing a Mozart piano sonata from memory, I lost my place a few minutes into the piece and wound up at the end before I'd played the middle. I was devastated—it was the first time I'd really bombed playing the piano. My parents tried to be supportive and kept talking about how good I'd sounded. I learned at that moment that some failures are best absorbed alone. I thanked them for their concern and spent the night replaying the disaster over and over. I knew that I hadn't really been prepared for the competition. Perhaps because playing the piano is both a physical and mental challenge, it's not possible to "cram" for a performance in the same way one can for an exam. In other words, practicing eight hours one day will not produce the same result as practicing one hour a day for eight days. I'd left my preparation to the last minute, and it showed.

A couple of days later I asked my piano teacher when the next competition would take place. It would be the Young Artists regional competition in the winter. I entered immediately. When my parents asked if it would help to practice on a grand piano, I spent weeks visiting piano stores trying to choose the right one to rent. All that preparation helped, and when I won the competition, my parents bought the piano. I learned later that they had to take out a $13,000 loan in order to do so. To this day, I still own and play that Chickering grand.

But while Daddy and I were doing very well, Mother was having a much more difficult time adjusting to Denver. She was unable to find a job right away, and for the first time I realized that my mother's sense of self was tied to her identity as a teacher. She really missed her family, particularly her mother, and we didn't have the money for frequent visits to Birmingham. To fill her days, Mother tried to throw herself into homemaking—even learning to make homemade bread, of all things. She made bread every week whether we ate it or not. At the age of fourteen I could see in my mother what it meant to make yourself content and happy, even if you were not fulfilled.

Mother also disliked the West's informality. One night shortly after moving we were invited to a cocktail party at the university. My mother dressed as she would have in Alabama, in semiformal attire. When we got there everyone was in pantsuits (polyester was the dominant fabric). Mother was clearly embarrassed, but when we got in the car she said, "Condoleezza, if you are overdressed, it is a comment on them. If you are underdressed, it is a comment on you." That statement has stayed with me over the years, and I have always dressed accordingly. But it said volumes about my mother and the importance she placed on social graces *and* nice clothes.

Despite this culture clash, the Rice family did settle into a rather comfortable life. Ice hockey became as important in our lives as football had been. The University of Denver had no football team, but it did have a tradition of championship hockey teams. We'd attended the games the year before, but now we purchased season tickets. Daddy became a member of the faculty athletic committee, which got us very good seats and a chance to get to know the hockey players. My parents liked the young men, most of whom were from western Canada, and treated them like surrogate sons, inviting them to dinner on many occasions. This was great for me since for the first time I was starting to react favorably to these creatures called boys.

chapter twenty

We were all looking forward to the coming hockey playoffs in March 1970. Denver was a powerhouse and stood a good chance of capturing their sixth national championship. I knew that Mother had a doctor's appointment that Friday but didn't think much of it.

Daddy always dropped me off at school each day and picked me up afterward; school ended about three-thirty. That Friday I waited and waited, and as more than an hour passed, I became concerned that something had happened to him. In those days, which were well before cell phones, there was no way to reach him. When he finally arrived, he explained that he'd been at the doctor's office. Mother had gone to Dr. Hamilton because she'd felt a lump in her breast, and she was still with the doctor, who was doing some tests.

When Daddy and I arrived at the doctor's office, the doctor explained that he couldn't be sure but the lump felt like cancer to him. In those days, you didn't wait for second opinions and analysis. Mother would have surgery on Monday morning. It was likely that she would lose her right breast, and then we'd see what else could be done.

That weekend was consumed with preparations for her hospital stay. I'll never forget the sight of Mother cooking and cooking, making and freezing chicken and beef roast and vegetables so that we would have enough to eat while she was hospitalized. I suspected she was trying to get her mind off what she was facing. In 1970, cancer was considered a death sentence. I could tell that she was scared. I could tell that Daddy was scared. And I was terrified. Not frightened in the same way that I'd been by the bombings in Birmingham. This cut much deeper. I could not conceive of life without my mother.

Mother was admitted to the hospital Sunday night. My parents decided that I should go to school that Monday. I think that was the longest day of my life. By the time I reached my one o'clock Latin class, I just couldn't wait any longer for news. I asked Mrs. Winters if I could go to the office and call my father, explaining that my mother was having surgery. I waited for what seemed like an hour in the principal's paneled office. Finally the nurses reached Daddy, and he said that the surgery was over and it was indeed a cancerous tumor. He asked if I wanted to leave school. I said yes, and he picked me up shortly after.

When we got to the hospital, Mother was awake and more relaxed than either my father or me. She was relieved to at least know the facts, and Dr. Hamilton was mildly encouraging that the cancer had been caught early. "Early" in those days meant that it had already spread to at least two lymph nodes. She'd need to undergo radiation therapy, which would start in the hospital and continue when she came home.

My father called my grandmothers, aunts, and uncles with the news. A steady parade of family began to descend upon us. My mother's sisters, brother, and sister-in-law all arrived. Grandmother Ray wisely stayed home. I love my extended family and we needed them, but after a while it felt like a bit of an intrusion. Mother stayed in the hospital about ten days. On the day before she was to leave, I arrived home from school to see my aunt Mattie moving the bedroom furniture around. "What are you doing?" I said. She explained that it was good when people came home from the hospital to have things look different. Certain that my mother wouldn't appreciate coming back to a rearrangement of her carefully decorated bedroom, I protested and insisted that the furniture be returned to its original position. My relatives stayed a few days longer. They were trying to help, and for a while they did buoy Mother's spirits. But then it was time for them to go home. Mother and Daddy and I just wanted to get back to normal. We needed to do that as a family, just the three of us. We even went to the hockey game the night the last relative left—only two weeks after my mother's surgery.

But when your mother is diagnosed with cancer you have to find a new normal. Once cancer enters your family's life it is a constant and unwelcome presence. I prayed every night that Mother's cancer would not come back. And there were Mother's periodic checkups, first every month, then every three, then every six, which provoked an indescribable anxiety as they approached and only temporary relief when they passed without incident. I once asked my mother, just before one of these periodic trips to the doctor, if she was afraid. "It's not so bad. I'm only nervous just before the doctor gives me the news," she responded. After five years, when cancer patients were thought to be "cured," we all celebrated. But frankly I never believed that the struggle was behind us, and I was right.

As the daughter of a mother who had breast cancer, I can confirm that the perpetual anxiety caused by a parent's disease is passed on to a child very directly. When Mother was first diagnosed in 1970, the genetic implications of the disease weren't as well understood as they are today. But over my lifetime the fact that my mother had breast cancer has persisted as a dominant factor in my own health prognosis. I started getting mammograms before I was thirty and have had several scary results leading to multiple biopsies. The promise of early detection (and the prayers that go with it) has become my talisman against this devastating disease.

The cancer altered Mother's life in other ways too. Though she never complained, I know that the drastic change in her physical appearance took a toll on her. Remember that this was a woman who took pride in her physical beauty and elegance. It was not standard practice then to do immediate reconstructive surgery after a mastectomy, and so Mother lived the rest of her life with a prosthetic bra. Moreover, the removal of several of her lymph nodes caused her left arm to swell to almost twice the size of her right. She covered the swelling by always wearing long-sleeved dresses. I remember one day when Mother went shopping and tried on a dress, the sleeve of which was too tight for her disfigured arm. The saleslady innocently asked what had happened. Mother addressed the situation directly, explaining that the swelling was the result of breast cancer surgery. The startled woman fumbled for something to say and then just said, "God bless you." Mother, gracious and calm, simply replied, "Thank you."

I learned a lot about Angelena Rice from how she faced these challenges. She didn't allow anything superficial to matter, brushing off the physical disfigurement and the psychological toll of living with the disease. She was grateful to be a survivor and to continue her life as wife and mother. Mother was strong in ways that I cannot to this day fully fathom and am certain that I couldn't reproduce. Her strength allowed us to go on with our lives.

My father was deeply affected too. He told me that his prayers had been answered. When he'd learned of my mother's diagnosis, he'd asked God not to take her, wondering, "How will I raise a fifteen-year-old alone?" He did not have to. Over the years, Daddy more often gave voice to his fears than Mother did, telling me, for example (but apparently not my mother), that the many doctors he'd spoken to had informed him that cancer never really goes away. "Those little seeds lie dormant and you never know when they'll strike again," he said. The fact is, from that brutal Monday forward our tight-knit family's sense of security was shaken by the infiltration of cancer into our consciousness. That was the new normal.

My great-grandfather was illiterate, but my great-grandmother, Julia Head, was a favored household slave who had learned to read as a young girl.

The son of sharecroppers, Granddaddy Rice received a scholarship to study at Stillman College after agreeing to become a Presbyterian minister. He was an "educational evangelist," establishing local schools and impressing upon his students the importance of attending college.

My father at three years old and his sister, Theresa, at five, shown here with my grandparents. Daddy was an easygoing personality and a superb athlete. Theresa was reclusive but brilliant.

My mother, Angelena (right), at three, and her sister, Mattie, at five. The cute little darlings were featured here as "calendar" girls for the local barbershop.

My maternal grandmother, Mattie Lula Parrom, had rich-brown skin and very high cheekbones, attesting to an ill-defined American Indian heritage. She is pictured here at her graduation from St. Mark's Academy, a "finishing" school for well-to-do young black women. RIGHT: After running away from home, my maternal grandfather, Albert Ray III, found himself alone in a train station one evening with just one token in his pocket. "Old Man Wheeler," the patriarch of a white family, brought him home and raised him with his sons.

Mother (far right), her brother, Alto, and her sister, Gee (far left) were often reminded by their parents to maintain their dignity despite the degrading circumstances of segregated Birmingham. They and their cousin, Kate, are pictured here with my grandfather's truck.

Daddy completed college and seminary at Johnson C. Smith University in North Carolina. Like his father, he would become an educational evangelist and mentor students in Birmingham, Tuscaloosa, Denver, and Palo Alto.

JOHN WESLEY RICE
Alpha Phi Alpha Fraternity
A.B. Major in Religious Education
Birmingham, Alabama
"*Our thoughts and conducts are our own.*"
Activities: Stillman Institute 1, 2; Y. M.C.A. 3, 4.

LEFT: My mother's students remembered her as an extraordinary beauty but also as a demanding teacher whom they obeyed despite her diminutive stature.

BELOW: Here I am sitting in Mother's lap, my little foot poking out from underneath the blanket. Had I been born a boy, my father would have named me John. But Mother got her way— a girl named Condoleezza, meaning "with sweetness."

Mother believed passionately in the importance of the arts and organized student-led performances wherever she taught. Here, the two of us pose for the cameras after one of her productions. It was late, and I was clearly ready to go home.

I started to play the piano at three. The little organ pictured here didn't have enough keys in the bass, so after I learned "What a Friend We Have in Jesus," my parents found the money one day to rent a real piano. I began to play at recitals throughout the city. Here I am playing for the new teachers' conference. I still don't understand my mother's decision to have me wear that fuzzy white hat.

LEFT: I spent the first three years of my life living with my parents in a small apartment in the back of Westminster Presbyterian, my father's church.

RIGHT: Mother and me, dressed in our swimsuits. I did not learn proper swimming techniques until I was twenty-five because Eugene "Bull" Connor closed Birmingham's recreational facilities after the courts ordered him to integrate them.

Here I am eyeing Santa Claus suspiciously. A few years later when we went to see Saint Nick, a racial incident almost broke out when my father noticed that the Santa in question was treating black and white children differently. Daddy was prepared to "pull all that stuff off him and expose him as just another cracker." Fortunately, Santa got the body language and treated me very well.

Pupil	Rice, Condoleezza						
Meaning of Marks A—Excellent B—Good C—Fair D—Poor (barely passing) F—Failure	1st Period 6 Weeks	2nd Period 6 Weeks	3rd Period 6 Weeks	4th Period 6 Weeks	5th Period 6 Weeks	6th Period 6 Weeks	Average
Days Present	29	26	32	29	26	34	164
Days Absent	3	7	1	1	5	2	13
Times Tardy	0	0	0	0	0	0	0
Conduct	A	A	A	A	A	A	
Arithmetic	A	A	A	A	A	A	
Art	C	B	C	C	C	C	C
Auditorium	B	A	B	A	A	A	
Geography	A	A	A	A	A	A	
Health	C	C	B	A	A	A	
History	C	A	A	A	A	A	
Home Economics							
Language	A	A	B	A	A	A	
Library	A	A	A	A	A	A	
Literature	B	A	A	B	A	A	
Manual Training							
Music	C	C	C	B	B	B	B
Physical Education	A	A	A	A	A	A	
Reading	A	A	A	A	A	A	
Safety	C	C	C	C	C	C	
Science	B	A	A	A	A	A	
Spelling	A	A	A	A	A	A	
Writing	B	B	B	A	A	B	B
Sunday School Credit	O	A	A	A	A	B	

Mother filled our home with beautiful, well-preserved mahogany furniture. The sofa on which my mother and I are sitting resides in my home today. *Courtesy of Chris McNair.* RIGHT: I liked but didn't love school. I got good grades despite a tendency toward procrastination. Clearly art (notice the string of Cs) was not my strong suit.

Here I am standing outside the White House during a family trip to D.C. My father said that I proclaimed, "I will work in there some day." I don't remember saying that, but my parents did have me convinced that even if I couldn't have a hamburger at Woolworth's lunch counter, I could grow up to be President of the United States.

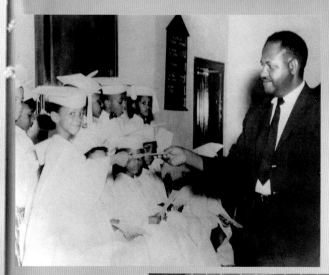

Daddy established a kindergarten program at his church. Here, at a "graduation" ceremony for his students, he is handing a diploma to Denise McNair, one of the four little girls who were killed in the Sixteenth Street Baptist Church bombing in 1963.

Courtesy of Chris McNair

Daddy's youth programs were renowned throughout the city. Here I am standing with members of Westminster's children's choir in the back row, second from the left.

December 11, 1961

Hon. Bull Connor
City Hall
B'ham, Ala.

Honorable Bull Connor:

I want to congratulate you for your actions in closing the city parks. I feel you acted in the best interest of all citizens of Ala., especially of Birmingham and Jefferson County.

Segregation is one of our most prized possessions, and we should maintain our prized possessions no matter what the price maybe.

Your decision in closing the city parks will go down in history.

I believe, your decision, will be praised by all white and most negroes of the South.

James W. Hartley

James W. Hartley

It was in 1961 that Eugene "Bull" Connor decided to close Birmingham's recreational facilities rather than integrate them. He received wide support from whites, like the author of this letter.

Eugene "Bull" Connor Papers, Birmingham, Alabama, Public Library Archives, Cat. #268.8.12.

Local civil rights leaders urged black customers to boycott white merchants who did not treat them equally. I was disappointed that we had to forgo our annual Christmas shopping but was old enough to understand the larger issues at stake.

Birmingham Civil Rights Institute

While the civil rights movement is remembered for nonviolent civil disobedience, that was not always the case. A full-scale riot erupted on May 11, 1963, with black protesters setting fire to police cars and confronting an armored personnel carrier rumored to contain Bull Connor himself. My parents and I went to survey the damage that next morning.

Associated Press

My school was selected to participate in the city's first integrated book fair at the Tutwiler Hotel. Here I am displaying my reading project. Mrs. Green, our teacher, was very proud to say that our presentations were far superior to the "shabby" ones of the white kids.

TOP LEFT: I took up figure skating while my parents pursued graduate work at the University of Denver. I was simply not very good. "It's amazing you can do a jump," one judge remarked. "You never actually leave the ice."

TOP RIGHT: The rigorous academics at St. Mary's Academy prepared me well for college. Life also revolved around trying to attract the boys at our brother schools, Mullen Prep and Regis High. Plaid skirts, bobby socks, and saddle shoes were part of the uniform.

Courtesy of St. Mary's Academy, 1969–1970 Yearbook

RIGHT: During my senior year at St. Mary's, Daddy "presented" me (top middle) at the Owl Club cotillion, a debutante ball for accomplished black high school girls. I felt totally out of place, since I had already transitioned to being a college student, taking classes at the University of Denver.

Courtesy of the Denver Public Library, Western History Collection; photo by Burnis McCloud

My father said that I couldn't live in the dorm because "he knew what went on in there." So I pledged Alpha Chi Omega. Here I am (back, right), pictured with my sisters.

Courtesy of the Archives and Special Collections, Penrose Library, University of Denver

RIGHT: As an assistant dean at the University of Denver, Daddy was the liaison to students during the raucous Vietnam War demonstrations, such as this one on Denver's Carnegie Field in 1971.

Courtesy of the Archives and Special Collections, Penrose Library, University of Denver

BELOW: I thought I'd found the man I wanted to marry, Rick Upchurch (center), a wide receiver for the Denver Broncos. He is pictured here with Rubin Carter, the Broncos' nose tackle, and my father, who is holding two-year-old Brian, the son of wide receiver Haven Moses and my good friend Joyce.

After deciding to abandon my dream of being a concert pianist, I wandered into a course in international politics taught by Josef Korbel (center). In one of those odd coincidences, the man who opened up the world of Soviet studies to me was the father of Madeleine Albright. Here I am (leaning forward) in Dr. Korbel's "Comparative Communism" class.

Courtesy of the Archives and Special Collections, Penrose Library, University of Denver

I received my PhD in August 1981 with a job offer from Stanford in hand. That morning, Daddy gave me a set of classic books that Granddaddy Rice had purchased during the Great Depression, despite his modest means. It remains one of the proudest moments of my life.

Stokely Carmichael (seated) was a regular speaker in my father's courses and even at an adult education seminar at virtually all-white Montview Boulevard Presbyterian Church in Denver. This radical black activist was a good friend of the family.

Courtesy of the Archives and Special Collections, Penrose Library, University of Denver

At Stanford, I developed a close circle of friends, including Randy Bean (center), Chip Blacker (left), and Louis Olave (right). My father loved Chip and Louis's dinners, followed by music played on Louis's amped-up stereo.

Courtesy of Chip Blacker and Louis Olave

Jendayi Frazer was a sophomore in one of my first classes at Stanford and, later, my first PhD student. She would go on to become the Africa specialist at the NSC, ambassador to South Africa, and the assistant secretary for African affairs at the State Department.

I first flew aboard Air Force One while working for President George H. W. Bush. Here is my maiden voyage in April 1989 on the way to the President's historic speech in Hamtramck, Michigan, welcoming revolutionary events in Poland.

George Bush Presidential Library and Museum

I first met Gen. Colin Powell while I was working for the Joint Chiefs of Staff at the Pentagon. He was serving as deputy national security advisor for President Reagan, and this first meeting gave rise to a friendship that I value to this day. *Office of the Joint Chiefs of Staff*

During one of our nightly phone conversations long after my mother's death, Daddy told me he planned to remarry. His intended bride was Clara Bailey, a principal in the Ravenswood School District. I couldn't have been happier for him, and I was thrilled to have the chance to travel back to California for the wedding.

When we scheduled the Malta Summit for December 1989, we didn't account for the weather. Here I am trying to hold on aboard the *Maxim Gorky*, a Soviet cruise ship.

Rice Personal Collection

BELOW: Here I am greeting Soviet leader Mikhail Gorbachev during the 1990 Washington Summit. Gorbachev was losing control of the revolution he had unleashed; the Soviet Union would cease to exist less than eighteen months after this picture was taken.

George Bush Presidential Library and Museum

A close mentor and friend, Gen. Brent Scowcroft (right) invited me to work at the National Security Council, where he served as national security advisor to President George H. W. Bush. Here we are toward the end of my service, standing with Brent's deputy, Bob Gates, who would later serve as secretary of defense.

George Bush Presidential Library and Museum

After returning to Stanford, I provided on-air commentary for ABC News about Soviet affairs. I was pleased to learn that the President, pictured here at Kennebunkport, was still interested in my advice.

George Bush Presidential Library and Museum

President Bush successfully led the United States and its allies through the uncharted territory of ending the Cold War. He and Mrs. Barbara Bush have been wonderful mentors and friends. Here we enjoy a common love of tennis while vacationing at his summer home in Maine.

Rice Personal Collection

Daddy was so proud to see his daughter working for the President of the United
States. Here we stand with President Bush and First Lady Barbara Bush in 1992.
George Bush Presidential Library and Museum

When I was Stanford's
provost, President
Gerhard Casper and
I led efforts to reform
undergraduate education,
establishing freshman
and sophomore seminars.
I loved teaching these
small classes, such as this
one on the Soviet Union.
*Copyright © Linda A. Cicero/
Stanford News Service*

When budget cuts forced
me to make difficult
decisions, Chicano
students set up a tent city
on the Quad and staged
a hunger strike. Here,
Gerhard (left) and I face
the students in front of
our offices.
*Copyright © Linda A. Cicero/
Stanford News Service*

Daddy served on the Board of Governors of the California Community Colleges. Today, annual fellowships are given in his honor, a fitting tribute to his life's work in education.

Courtesy of the Chancellor's Office, California Community Colleges; photo by Sam Wood

ABOVE: Gene Washington, best known as a former NFL wide receiver, remains one of my closest friends to this day.

LEFT: I have been blessed with a wonderful extended family, including (from left to right) Will Alston, my uncle Alto, my aunt Connie, my cousin Lativia, Aunt Gee, my stepbrother, Greg, and my stepmother, Clara.

In 1992, Susan Ford Dorsey and I tapped several other community leaders and launched an after-school enrichment program for disadvantaged children in nearby East Palo Alto. We called it the Center for a New Generation, and it thrives today as a part of the Boys and Girls Clubs of America.

Courtesy of the Boys and Girls Club of the Peninsula

chapter twenty-one

Through the spring and summer of 1970 life was once again taken up with piano, skating, and school. My first major figure-skating competition, held that August, was relatively successful—I wound up finishing third. Many years later I teased my parents about having put me in the wrong sport—I was five foot seven with the long legs of someone who was five foot ten, and that was exactly the wrong body type to get any leverage for jumping. "I should have been a tennis player," I told them. They reminded me that it was I who'd wanted to be a figure skater.

That summer competition was the only one in which I ever placed. I was simply not a very good skater. In any case, I loved the challenge, and the sport taught me discipline and perseverance. I have often said that skating taught me more about character than the piano did. It's really difficult to work hard, fail at the moment of truth, and have to get up and work at it the next day. But that is precisely what skating taught me to do. It may be why my parents continued to pour money into my obviously limited potential on the ice and why my father got up every morning and took me to the rink before dawn.

I'd settled into a very nice life and didn't think much of it when my parents said one day after school that they wanted to talk about college. I assumed they meant that it was time to think about applying to universities, since I was entering my senior year. But they had something else in mind.

We sat in the living room, my mother on the sofa, Daddy in the pink chair, and I on the piano bench. This put us in a semicircle so that our eyes met very directly. Daddy seemed quite hesitant. He started the conversation by noting that I had almost completed the requirements for graduation at St. Mary's. This was true, but I was planning to take a set of Advanced Placement courses and work extra hard on my piano the next year. I had my eye on entering and finishing conservatory and then going to study in Europe.

Daddy said that he'd been talking to people at the university and that it might be possible for me to skip my senior year and begin my college curriculum there. This would allow me more time for piano as well. He knew that I wanted to apply to a music conservatory, perhaps Juilliard in New York or the Curtis Institute of Music in Philadelphia. But, he said, this was risky, since once I was in a conservatory I wouldn't be able to change my mind and major in something else. Moreover, I had a lot of interests, and Daddy and my mother thought that I would be unhappy in a conservatory.

I protested that I really wanted to be a musician and that they knew this. Was this just a way to keep me in Denver? This retort came out rather bluntly, but I'd long suspected that my parents did not want me to leave home. It was true that I was pretty young. But I believed that they just couldn't imagine sending me off to college and breaking up our tight-knit threesome. For the first time in my life I felt that this was more about them than about me, and I resented it.

Mother said nothing when I leveled this charge. Daddy remained calm and explained that I could always transfer after one year at Denver if I really wanted to but that they felt strongly that I should forgo my senior year at St. Mary's. I could go to Denver practically tuition free thanks to a deep discount for the children of faculty. I said I'd think about it, but I didn't like the idea.

Several days later I came back with a counterproposal. This time they sat on the sofa and I stood the entire time. I told them that I'd thought about it and had come up with a good idea. Why not finish my senior year in high school and start my freshman year in college at the same time? I wanted to finish with my high school class but was attracted to getting a jump on college.

My parents explained that St. Mary's cost a lot of money. I selfishly said that I knew that but wasn't prepared to give up my senior year. I remember this as one of the most unpleasant conversations I ever had with my parents. They stood their ground and I stood mine. I know that I was angry, and I suspect that they were too.

The next day we talked again, and after some back-and-forth they agreed to my idea. We set about designing a hybrid path. Each day I would skate and go to DU until eleven o'clock. Then I'd head over to St. Mary's, where I'd take only a couple of required courses and practice the piano. After that I'd go home to study, skate, and practice the piano some more before bedtime.

This worked for exactly one quarter. I've always needed more in my life than success at work, and I quickly found that I didn't belong socially to either St. Mary's or the university. The final year is supposed to be a bonding year for seniors, but I was rarely around for any of the activities and was largely excluded from various committees and class offices. Some of my teachers resented my attending the university, taking it as an affront to the quality of their teaching. When I proudly showed my first college English paper, for which I'd received an A, to a teacher at St. Mary's, she grumpily dismissed it as not very good or worthy of an A in her Advanced Placement course. St. Mary's made it quite clear that my college grades wouldn't be counted toward my academic standing. There was no chance that I would be valedictorian.

I knew that something had to give, but I was bound and determined not to admit to my parents that they'd been right—especially given the high tuition they were paying. So I decided that I'd complete the hybrid year but that I was going to have to find footing in one world or the other. It would be easier to go forward than to go back, I reasoned. That meant really becoming a college student.

First I had to free up some time. I was tired of getting up every morning at four-thirty and never being able to go out with my new college friends for pizza or a burger. So I quit competitive skating that spring, continuing to skate but at a greatly reduced level. Second, I started spending what free time I had at the university, going to St. Mary's only for my classes. Since I had turned sixteen and now could drive, traveling back and forth was much easier. My life began to revolve around the university and my new friends—many of them hockey players in whom I had more than a passing interest as potential boyfriends.

St. Mary's receded more and more into the background. I'd been fifteen at the time of my junior prom and not yet dating, so my father had arranged for his secretary's brother to take me to the dance. He was a nice young man, but I decided that night that I was never again going to a big dance with someone my father had chosen. When senior prom rolled around, I asked one of the hockey players. He went with me, but the poor guy—a college boy—was so uncomfortable at a high school prom that we left early.

The social strains of being so young and so advanced in school had finally caught up with me. I was now barely sixteen and a freshman in college. My parents were concerned too. They worried that I was suddenly hanging out with a crowd much older and far more mature than I was. Nineteen seventy-one was a time of sex, drugs, and rock and roll. When I announced that I wanted to move to campus for my sophomore year they came unglued. My father said that I'd never live in the dorms because he was a university administrator and "knew what went on in there."

My mother added her two cents. "You are just too young to be hanging out with these people. What could they possibly want from you except to take advantage of you?"

I hit the roof. "This early college enrollment was *your* idea," I said. "Now you're going to have to live with the consequences and trust that I'm smarter than you think I am."

This was the biggest fight my parents and I had ever had. Looking back on it, I see that they had set in motion events that challenged me to grow up very fast. I think they believed that I could advance in school and remain their little girl socially. But I was not one of those prodigies who had no social skills and no social life. I loved to have friends, and for better or worse, my friends were now college kids.

In response to my father's retort about the dorms, I asked him what he thought of the sorority houses. I don't think he saw what was coming and said that the Greek houses were a lot better. "Okay, then I'll join a sorority," I told them, and I did. I pledged Alpha Chi Omega. I loved the house and spent much of my free time there, learning to play bridge, planning social functions, and becoming a little sister of the fraternity Lambda Chi Alpha.

One of the truly anticlimactic days of my life was high school graduation. The school didn't even spell my name correctly on my diploma. My mother, who sixteen years before had put so much work into creating that name, sent the diploma back so that "Condoleezza" would be spelled properly, with two zs. The diploma wasn't returned until years later, when some members of the State Department press corps, having heard the story, petitioned St. Mary's for a replacement as a departure gift when I stepped down as secretary of state in 2009.

chapter twenty-two

As it turned out, I didn't move immediately into the sorority house. It did finally begin to dawn on me how much money my parents had been and were still investing in me. Time was running out on our lease in university housing, which expired after two years. I knew that my parents couldn't afford new housing *and* room and board for me on campus. So I relented and joined them in hunting for a house for us. I learned many years later that Vice Chancellor Blackburn had tried to get my father to buy a house. Daddy told him that they couldn't afford to because "Condoleezza is our house." My parents' investment in me meant that they had no choice but to adopt the itinerant lifestyle of my paternal grandparents rather than that of my mother's landowning family. They would occupy four different rental properties before finally buying a house in 1979, ten years after moving to Denver. The fact is, my parents probably never made more than

$60,000 a year between them. In retrospect, I wish I'd been smart enough to understand that at the time and found a way to relieve some of the financial pressure.

One of my father's friends had seen a house for rent in a neighborhood not too far from the university. It sounded perfect: three bedrooms and a large living room to accommodate my grand piano. When you own a grand piano it's like having a child or a pet. You have to have the right place for it, and this was always a major consideration in house hunting.

When we met the landlady at the door, I could tell that she was anxious and acting strangely. After showing the house, she said that she had some other people who were likely to rent it. That would have been an acceptable explanation, but she went on to say that she couldn't rent it in any case to someone who owned a piano because it might disturb the neighborhood. It was a dead giveaway. She was finding an excuse not to rent to us because we were black. Somehow when you grow up in Alabama you can spot racism at a hundred paces. My parents and I knew immediately what was happening.

My father challenged her. The house had been available only a day before when his friend had seen it. It didn't make sense to rule out pianos. Did any of the neighbors have stereos? Maybe some even had pianos? "You don't want to rent to us because we're black," he told her. "And now nothing that you do can convince us to rent this house. But I hope you'll enjoy dealing with the equal housing suit that we are about to file."

The woman almost fell over backward. No, no, she had

just heard complaints in the neighborhood about music, she explained. We were such a nice family. Our piano would be no problem. My parents and I left and we didn't file suit. My father said that the threat had accomplished its purpose because she'd never discriminate again. He would explain to Dr. Blackburn what had happened, and he was sure that Blackburn would extend our lease in university housing. Daddy went on to say that racism was clearly alive and well in Denver in 1972 and that he preferred the blatant racism of Alabama, for in the South, "at least you knew where you stood."

I understood that sentiment because I'd experienced this implicit racism firsthand. There was, of course, the incident with my guidance counselor, in which she advised me to try junior college. And then in my freshman Introduction to Government course, the professor had given a lecture on theories of racial superiority professed by social scientists such as William Shockley, who posited that blacks had lower IQs because of nature, not nurture. The professor had given the lecture under the guise of simply introducing us to the literature, but I sensed that he bought into some of the theory. I was the youngest person in the class, but I challenged him. "I speak French and play Bach. I'm better in your culture than you are," I said. "That shows that these things can be taught!" He was angry and said the next day that I had tried to silence him. I thought this was a ridiculous exchange between a senior professor and a college freshman. But I persisted, and finally I went to the dean and complained, mostly to create a record should the professor decide to retaliate. After a few days the professor asked to see me and then went on to compound the problem by drawing a little graph charting black IQs along the bottom, with those of whites above them. "But sometimes there are people like you," he said. He then showed my IQ line positioned above both, saying that I was special. Clearly, he didn't get the point. I left determined to ace his exam, which I did. He told me that he'd be glad to be a reference for me at any time. I'd made my point but obviously never asked for his help.

In this way, Denver was an odd departure from Alabama. On the surface everything was just fine, fully integrated. But underneath—occasionally in a college class, or when we looked for housing, or in my high school guidance counselor's reaction to my low standardized test scores—there was racism, perhaps unconscious and certainly unacknowledged. We hadn't left racism behind in Alabama. And in some ways this less explicit form of prejudice was more insidious and harder to confront.

Many years later, when I was asked about my decision to become a Republican, I first explained quite honestly that the choice reflected my disgust with Jimmy Carter's foreign policy and my attraction to Ronald Reagan's worldview. But, pressed about the domestic agenda of the two parties, I gave an answer that came directly from my experience with the many forms racism can take. "I would rather be ignored than patronized," I said, pointing to the tendency of the Democratic Party to talk about "women, minorities, and the poor." I hated identity politics and the self-satisfied people who assumed that they were free of prejudice when, in fact, they too could not see beyond color to the individual.

Race is a constant factor in American life. Yet reacting to

every incident, real or imagined, is crippling, tiring, and ultimately counterproductive. I'd grown up in a family that believed you might not control your circumstances but you could control your reaction to them. There was no room for being a victim or depending on "the white man" to take care of you. That self-sufficiency is the ethos passed down by my ancestors on both sides of the family, and I have internalized it thoroughly. Despite the gross inequities my ancestors faced, there *has* been progress, and today race no longer determines how far one can go. That said, America is not color-blind and likely never will be.

chapter twenty-three

After the housing incident we did indeed stay in a university-owned home for another year. Mother was hired by the university as an admissions officer and threw herself into this new opportunity with great enthusiasm. She was good at it, too, receiving reams of thank-you letters from prospective candidates and their parents whom she helped. I was so happy for her because finally she had her professional life back.

Daddy earned accolades for his work at the university as well. My father's touch with young people easily translated across racial boundaries, and he became at Denver, as he had at Stillman, one of the best-known figures on campus. The university administration relied on Daddy for difficult tasks. When the shootings of students protesting the Vietnam War took place at Kent State University in 1970, Denver, like virtually every other campus, erupted in protests and sit-ins.

My father became the university's liaison to the students, helping to calm the situation. I wasn't particularly caught up in the political fervor but did attend one rally on Carnegie Field where my father proclaimed to the crowd, "It seems to me as if we need a demonstration to end all demonstrations!" Somewhere there is a picture of me sitting with the student demonstrators looking up at him on the stage.

The truth is that music majors were so busy with practice, rigorous and difficult theory classes, and performance demands that there wasn't much time for anything else. When I accepted a post as news editor of DU's student newspaper, the *Clarion*, I quickly learned that I simply didn't have enough time for extracurricular activities—I couldn't stay at the paper all night with my colleagues, reading copy and producing the paper. Eventually I quit, or perhaps I was fired. I quite honestly can no longer remember the circumstances.

I constantly clashed with the music faculty, which rightly didn't think me single-minded enough in my devotion to piano. After one fairly poor performance before the entire piano faculty, my teacher suggested that I rededicate myself to the piano by going to the Aspen Music Festival School that summer of my sophomore year. I did, and I knew I'd become a far better pianist that summer. And I also knew that no matter how much better I became or how hard I worked, I'd never be good enough. The many prodigies studying there, some not yet into their teens, gave me a glimpse of the barriers to a concert career. I left Aspen having experienced a crisis of confidence and returned home to Denver set on finding a new path.

I asked to talk to my parents. We sat in the living room,

they on the sofa and I on the piano bench. I told them that I wanted to change my major. I hated the single-minded focus of the piano program and had determined that I'd never be good enough to rise to the top of the profession. "It's not good enough to have a career teaching thirteen-year-olds to murder Beethoven," I told them.

They knew me better than anyone else, but they hadn't seen this coming. At first my dad suggested that I change my major from the very demanding bachelor of music (the performance degree) to the broader bachelor of arts in music, which meant that I could take a number of courses in other departments. I explained that this wasn't just about the narrowness of the degree. "I've played the piano since I was three," I said. "But I don't love it enough to end up as a music teacher, and that's where I'm headed."

"What are you changing your major to?" Daddy asked.

"I don't know. Just not music," I said.

"You're going to end up as a waitress at Howard Johnson's because you don't know what you want to do with your life," he responded. I don't know why he picked on Howard Johnson's, and after all, he'd once waited tables himself, but this was as powerful a rebuke as he could muster. I was accustomed to having my parents support me in everything I did, so my father's response was truly shocking.

"I'd rather be a waitress at Howard Johnson's than teach piano. And after all, it's my life."

"It's our money," Daddy retorted.

Mother intervened. "Come on, Rice, that's not fair." She looked back at me. "What your father is saying is that you're already a junior in college and you don't know what you want to do. You need to find a major or you won't graduate on time," she said calmly.

That evening I asked Mother why she wasn't upset about my decision. More than anyone else, she'd been responsible for my love of music and my pursuit of a career in it. I would never fulfill that dream. Mother just smiled and said, "Do you remember when I told you that you weren't old enough or good enough to quit?" I laughed, recalling that moment. "Now you are old enough *and* good enough. For the rest of your life your piano will always be there for you." When I had the chance many years later, as national security advisor, to play with the great cellist Yo-Yo Ma, and then as secretary of state, for the Queen of England, I knew how wise my mother had been.

I did eventually find a major. After false starts in English literature and political science with a focus on state and local government, I was getting pretty desperate by the spring of my junior year. That's when I wandered into an introductory course on international politics taught by a man named Josef Korbel. Korbel had been a Czech diplomat during World War II and had successfully mediated the 1948 Kashmir crisis for the United Nations before settling in Denver and founding the Graduate School of International Studies. He opened up an entirely new world to me. I loved his stories about the work of diplomats. He was a specialist on the Soviet Union, and I was quickly drawn into his tales of the byzantine intrigue of Josef Stalin. At the end of the quarter, I asked to see him and told him that I wanted to be a Soviet specialist and study international politics. He encouraged me to do so, saying that he had a daughter who was studying at

Columbia. Her name was Madeleine Albright and perhaps we could meet someday.

When I went home and told my parents that I'd found what I wanted to do, they were really happy. If they had any doubts about the wisdom of a nice black girl from Alabama studying the Soviet Union, they didn't express them, though in retrospect I'm sure they had plenty. "Jump on it with four feet," my father said. And I did. I declared myself a political science major and started studying the Russian language. I had found my passion, or more accurately, it had found me. In any case, I finally knew what I loved, though I frankly didn't know where it would lead me. I remember being particularly conscious of starting down a path that was very different from anything in my parents' experience. They had always been there for me and always would be. But I would have to navigate my professional life on my own. That brought an unexpected sense of maturity and newfound freedom.

chapter twenty-four

The remainder of my college time seemed to fly by. I worked in the summer of my junior year and during Christmas break as a temporary secretary at the university. I had to type purchasing requisitions, which required six carbon copies. If you made a mistake, you had to start all over again since there was no way to correct the carbons. As awful as the job was, it allowed me finally to help with the financial demands on the family. Thus, in the fall of my senior year, my parents and I agreed that I could move into the sorority house. I'd live apart from them for the first time in my life. That Saturday in mid-September when we loaded up the car with my clothes, a new bedspread for my room, and several other personal items, it seemed like a huge step—despite the fact that the sorority house was located about five minutes from where my parents lived.

Of course, the distance seemed much greater. I felt a good

deal of personal freedom and exercised it. There were some constraints because Daddy was so well known on campus. Yet I managed to allow tendencies toward procrastination to take full flight. Fortunately, the political science classes were much easier than music and I didn't need to work as hard.

Early in the year, I learned that I needed surgery on my hand to remove a ganglion cyst, which meant that I couldn't study piano for several months. I quit skating altogether and gained thirty pounds due to the lack of exercise and a sudden affinity for the International House of Pancakes. This time, despite the extra pounds, when I needed a date for the sorority formal, I didn't have to rely on my father to find one. Rich Preston, the captain of the hockey team and my first real crush, took me to the dance. The night turned out to be a little tense, though, since the hockey game in which Rich was playing went into overtime while I sat at the sorority house waiting. I was relieved when my father called to say that the game had ended and that Rich was on his way.

I also used my expanded free time to become deeply involved in student government and service activities with the sorority, resulting in my selection that spring as Denver University's Outstanding Senior Woman. (A few years before, the award had carried the politically incorrect title of Miss DU.)

Throughout this period, my parents and I were developing a new kind of relationship. We still met every Saturday night for dinner followed by the hockey game. And I found it useful to drop in on them during the week, bringing my laundry with me. We also established a pattern that we kept until the end of their lives: we talked on the telephone every night.

That fall, I started to think seriously about the next chapter in my life. Here, my parents and I were in complete agreement that at age nineteen, I was probably too young to do anything but continue in school. In any case, I had come to political science so late that I needed another year of academic training to pursue my interest in the Soviet Union.

I applied to several graduate schools to study politics and economics and was accepted everywhere except Penn State. Denver was on my list as a fallback, but I never intended to stay at the university. I wanted to go to Notre Dame, which offered a very good program in Soviet studies and encouraged a strong concentration in economics as well. We'd visited South Bend when I was a sophomore in college and I'd loved it. My parents wanted me to stay in Denver, but if that was not possible, they said Notre Dame was a great choice.

One afternoon in April, my father drove up in his red Ford as I came out of the sorority house on my way to class. He stopped at the corner and said, "I have something for you." Daddy handed me the letter from Notre Dame graduate school admissions, which had come to my parents' house. I took a deep breath and opened the letter. The news was good—I was in. Daddy started to get out of the car, so excited that he forgot to put it in park. After quickly securing the brake, my father, all six feet two inches and 260 pounds of him, leapt out and hugged me. I think he was prouder of me than I was of myself, and to this day that is one of my fondest memories of him.

After I was admitted to Notre Dame, I relaxed and enjoyed the remainder of my senior year. The spring and summer were dominated by the Watergate scandal and Richard

Nixon's subsequent resignation. My friends in the sorority, unlike the music majors I'd left behind, were also riveted by the proceedings. We'd sprint home from class every day to watch the testimony on TV.

One of the jobs that I had taken on at the university was director of the student speakers bureau. We had invited Bob Woodward, the crusading young *Washington Post* reporter, to speak one evening in May, but he had to cancel on the day of the speech. I was angry with him, but my anger evaporated when later that day another student showed me a newspaper headline: "President Hands Over Transcripts: Initial Reaction on Hill Divided Along Party Lines." For the first time, all 1,254 pages of the Nixon Watergate papers were to be made public to the Congress and the American people, and Woodward was intimately involved in working on the story. I subsequently related this tale to Woodward and reminded him of the trouble he'd caused in my life (not for the last time) when I was a senior at DU.

Finally it was graduation day, and as the Outstanding Senior Woman, a.k.a. Miss DU, I led the processional. My father, who'd been promoted to assistant vice chancellor that year, marched with the faculty not too far behind. The celebration was very nice but not very memorable. There was so much ahead. I was just starting my life. Thinking back, I'm reminded of that wonderful line in the Barbra Streisand and Robert Redford movie *The Way We Were* when Streisand says, "Commencement. What a funny thing to call the end."

chapter twenty-five

Throughout the summer of 1974, my parents and I were consumed with preparations for my impending move to South Bend. As part of that, I went back to skating and ballet to lose the thirty pounds that I'd put on during my senior year. My mother helped by cooking only healthy foods, leading my father to complain that he didn't really like dinners where "green things were the centerpiece of the meal."

I could tell, though, that the prospect of my really leaving home for the first time, perhaps never to return, was starting to trouble my mother. Tensions would rise between us over the smallest things. One such incident still bothers me to this day. I'd gone to a sorority sister's wedding on Father's Day of that year. My parents and I had planned to have dinner together to celebrate the holiday, but the wedding reception ran very long and it was far away in the outskirts of Denver. When I finally returned home, well after dinnertime,

CONDOLEEZZA RICE

my mother was furious, declaring that I was showing a lack of respect for their feelings. I countered that I'd called to say that I would be late and couldn't do anything about my sisters—and hence my ride—wanting to stay until the bridal bouquet was thrown.

My father called me into my bedroom and said that he fully understood what had happened but that this was a new phase for the whole family and asked if I could be "a little more sensitive" to my mother's feelings. It occurred to me that my mother and father had grown up very differently in this regard. My father had left home at eighteen, never to return. My mother, on the other hand, had lived at home until she married at twenty-nine. She didn't know what it was like to go off to college, and she was having a difficult time watching her daughter break up the family group—even if it was a perfectly natural thing to do.

The day of my departure for Notre Dame finally came. My parents took me to the airport and waved goodbye at the gate. Mother was, as expected, very emotional. Daddy was mostly worried about whether I would be able to navigate the change of planes in Chicago—not a crazy concern given the complications of O'Hare even in that day. He was reassured when I told him that I was planning to meet my college roommates' families during the layover.

When I called the next day I told my parents that all had gone well. In fact, it hadn't, and I got off to a rocky start. I arrived at the tiny South Bend airport after it had closed down for the night. The plane from Chicago had been late and South Bend wasn't, in those days, a hub of activity in any case. There was no one at the desk and no apparent means of transportation to the university. I was a little panicked, but then I saw another young woman who looked lost too and asked if she might by any chance be trying to get to Notre Dame. "Yes," she said, obviously relieved to have found a companion. We tracked down the only cab driver still at the airport. He took pity on us, despite the fact that he was preparing to go home for the night, and drove us to Notre Dame.

The next day I went out to find a few things to furnish my room. My parents had given me a new car for graduation, an Oldsmobile Omega, which I'd named Boris, after my favorite Russian opera, *Boris Godunov*. Boris had a tendency to overheat and did so that day in the August heat and humidity of South Bend. I pulled to the side and walked across the street to the service station. The attendant said sharply, "You'll have to bring it over here." I took offense. When I asked even more pointedly why he couldn't go across the street and fix it, he said very meekly, "I thought it might cool off quicker in the shade over here."

I'd reacted in this way because South Bend in particular, but also Indiana, had a reputation for racism. My father had reminded me that the emergence of the modern-day Ku Klux Klan had occurred in Indiana, not Dixie. To avoid problems, a fellow student at Notre Dame had told me to find the biggest Fighting Irish sticker I could and put it on the rear window of my car. "They leave Notre Dame students alone," he said. I was conditioned to expect trouble and viewed the gas station attendant's response through that prism. After that incident, however, I decided that I was going to give people in South Bend the benefit of the doubt. And thankfully, I never had another problem with anyone. To this day, I think back on that rush to judgment whenever I am tempted to see racism in a rebuff.

Later that day as I was moving boxes into my room, a nice young man asked if I needed help. I was immediately attracted to Wayne Bullock, the Notre Dame fullback. When I asked what I could do for him, he said he wanted chocolate chip cookies. Soon I was standing in the kitchen of Lewis Hall, the convent that doubled as the graduate women's dormitory on campus, trying to make sense of a Toll House cookie recipe, when I encountered another PhD student named Jane Robinett who seemed to know what to do. Jane became my big sister and my best friend at Notre Dame, and we have remained close ever since.

Wayne and I began to see each other, though I knew that he had a "hometown honey." He was a bruising fullback with a heart of gold whose greatest desire was to play pro football and start a family so that he could have lots of kids. When my parents came to visit South Bend that fall, my father fell in love with Wayne. He was my dad's kind of running back, tough and relentless. And he was my dad's kind of guy, sweet and solid. It seemed that every time I called home, Daddy asked about Wayne and was sorely disappointed to learn that the relationship wasn't progressing. When my parents came back in the spring, Daddy was disturbed to find that Wayne was no longer on the scene. I'd dated Randy Payne, another nice guy, for a while, but my new love was a six-foot-five middle linebacker who wore a bandana around his head and an earring in his ear. "He looks like a thug," Daddy said.

Not surprisingly, I took offense, reminding my father that

he shouldn't judge people by how they looked. After all, I was experimenting with bell-bottoms and platform shoes. Daddy didn't say much after that, but he clearly hoped that I'd find "a nice boy." It was obvious by then that we didn't share the same criteria for a mate. My mother gently reminded Daddy that the young John Wesley Rice Jr. had been a bit of a rogue too—dancing and playing cards, smoking cigarettes and drinking whiskey. "And you were a *preacher*," she added.

Graduate school was challenging enough but not really difficult. The work in the government department confirmed my interest in Soviet studies, but I found the classes in economics more exciting. Many years later I'd take up the study of military affairs because it was more concrete. Militaries have weapons that you can see, budgets that you can quantify, and doctrine that you can read. Studying the politics of the Soviet Union meant trying to divine what Leonid Brezhnev might have said to Alexei Kosygin from little clues in Russian newspapers. It was not for me. Fortunately, one of the professors in the economics department took me under his wing and helped me understand how to use quantitative methods in the study of political and economic phenomena. I was pretty good at math and found econometrics and statistics useful. It was akin to doing the complicated theory problems that I'd encountered in music. I received all As at Notre Dame, but despite the faculty's encouragement, I decided not to pursue a PhD in economics. I thoroughly enjoyed South Bend but decided that I would return to Denver. I thought that I should, for the first time in my life, *get a job*!

chapter twenty-six

I returned to Denver late in the summer of 1975, full of expectations that my new master's degree would help me land an interesting job. My parents were delighted to have me back home, and invited me to redecorate my room. I did so in the style of the mid-1970s, complete with a gauzy red and pink Indian print bedspread and lots of candles purchased from Pier 1 Imports. Nonetheless, I told my folks that I intended to stay for only a year or so until I could afford my own place.

A friend from Notre Dame called to say that her boyfriend, who'd been drafted by the Denver Broncos, was planning to go out after the Broncos' first exhibition game with some of his friends and wondered if I'd be willing to come along. I agreed to go, and after the game we met up with several of his rookie friends. The night was a disaster. The players were a bit loud for my taste—and cheap. We went dancing at a bar, but they ran out of money, leaving the girls to pay for the third and fourth rounds of drinks (though they seemed to find money for a stop at McDonald's on the way home). The evening seemed to go on forever, and I was really glad to finally get home well after two in the morning.

The next day my friend called to say that one of the guys who'd seen me the evening before wanted to meet me. "You are just lucky that I'm speaking to you," I told her, reminding her of how badly the night had gone. But she persisted, saying that Rick Upchurch hadn't been among the offending group and was really nice. The four of us went out, and I found myself very attracted to Rick, who was a fourth-round draft choice from the University of Minnesota.

The next day I ran to the grocery store to look up his name in *Street & Smith's* pro football guide. Frankly, I wanted to see if he was likely to make the team and stick around for a while. As I was returning home from the store, Rick drove up in his new blue and white Chevy. He met my parents, who were very impressed with his politeness. We started seeing each other regularly, almost every day.

Rick was a good guy, and for the first time I thought I'd found the man I wanted to marry. We were so in sync, and he loved my parents. I came home one evening to find Rick in the basement playing pool with my father. It wasn't uncommon for Rick to visit my dad even when I was not there.

My personal life was very satisfying, but I couldn't find a job. The economy was in recession in 1975, and I quickly learned that my Soviet studies expertise wasn't very much in demand in Denver. I considered moving to Washington, D.C., but I didn't want to leave Rick and my very happy life in Denver. I decided to teach piano, the one thing for which there was demand. The irony was not lost on me, or my parents, that the very thing I'd feared had come to pass: I was a piano teacher.

One evening my father came into my room where I was listening to sad songs and feeling very much the failure. He told me that he was sure the setback was temporary but wondered if I'd acquired enough education to do what I wanted to do. He knew that I'd applied to law school and been accepted at several, including Denver. "Do you want to be a lawyer?" he asked. I said no but that I was sure a law degree would mean something in the workplace. I certainly didn't want to chase a PhD. I could have added, *And end up like Aunt Theresa, reading the same book twenty-five times.* "Well," Daddy said, "your mother and I are ready to help you in whatever you decide to do." He didn't have to say it, but I was glad that he did.

Then one day shortly before Christmas I went by to say hello to Dr. Korbel. I hadn't done so since returning from Notre Dame. The afternoon was snowy and cold and Dr. Korbel was sitting in his corner office in his cardigan sweater, smoking the pipe that he almost always seemed to have with him. He asked what I was doing and in an instant I poured out everything to him. I wanted to be a Soviet specialist, but I didn't want to take on PhD work. Maybe I would go to law school, but I didn't want to be a lawyer. "Frankly," I told him, "I don't know what I want to do."

Over the years I've seen so many of my students go through this crisis of confidence. Having been through it myself has helped me be a better advisor. And I have told countless students what both my father and Dr. Korbel told me: "If you don't want to be a lawyer, don't go to law school."

So I didn't. Dr. Korbel helpfully suggested that I just take a few courses starting that winter quarter. I wouldn't have to commit to a PhD program but could see if I still liked the idea of more graduate work. I learned that there was a master's degree in public administration, which sounded practical, and I thought I might enter that program in the spring. I started classes and was so happy to be back in school.

That winter Aunt Theresa came to visit. One day she asked if I was happy doing graduate work, adding that I seemed to be even if it wasn't leading anywhere. She related the ups and downs of her journey, including her experience as a visiting professor at the University of Liberia in 1961. It started to occur to me that she had indeed had an interesting career. And then she said something that had a lasting impact on me: "Condoleezza, if you don't do the PhD you'll always wonder how far you could have gone."

I thought hard about it, consulted Dr. Korbel again, and before the spring quarter ended was admitted to the PhD program at the Graduate School of International Studies at Denver. And oh yes, I continued to teach piano, but with a new purpose: it helped pay my graduate school bills.

chapter twenty-seven

Rick Upchurch went back to the University of Minnesota to finish college after the football season. He was therefore away when I resumed my academic career. When he returned for training camp in the summer it was clear that things had changed. We started dating again, still speaking of commitment to one another. But Rick had complications in his life—certain obligations that he needed to take care of. He was and still is one of the best human beings I've ever known, but as a friend of ours put it, he had "too many irons in the fire." Our relationship ended gently and we remained friends.

In the fall of 1976, Ambassador Horace Dawson, one of the highest-ranking blacks in the Foreign Service, asked my father to serve on an external review of the United States Information Agency. We decided that this would provide me with good exposure to Washington. So my mother and I accompanied my father for the six-week assignment. Since

Denver didn't start until late September, I missed only two weeks of school. It was worth it because Horace Dawson became a mentor and friend and remains so to this day. He insisted that I apply for an internship at the State Department for the coming summer. I did and would soon receive my first paying job in international relations.

In general, things could not have been better at Denver. I began to prepare for doctoral qualifying exams, and to satisfy the requirement of a thesis-length research paper, I wrote on politics and music in the Soviet Union, exploring the impact of the totalitarian policies of Josef Stalin on composers such as Prokofiev and Shostakovich. I had finally found a way to unite my interests in music and politics.

Then, early in the spring quarter of 1977, Dr. Korbel asked to see me. He looked awful, and I noticed that his usually ruddy complexion had an undeniably yellow cast. Dr. Korbel said that he would be going into the hospital that afternoon and wondered if I'd take over his undergraduate course. The quarter had just begun, and I told him that of course I would take the class until he could return. He said that he didn't know when that would be. The conversation really unnerved me. As it turned out, the class was a lot of work and I didn't really love the teaching. But I did a creditable job and was pleased to have the experience on my resume.

Soon after, I left for my internship at the State Department. It was so exciting to move into my first apartment. I realize now that it was pretty dumpy, but it was my first and I loved it. The internship itself was pretty boring. I was assigned to the Bureau of Educational and Cultural Affairs, working on a project examining Soviet cultural programs in the Third World. Toward the end I worked on the somewhat more pressing issue of the education of Cuban soldiers in the Soviet Union.

On balance, the internship was a good experience largely because the people for whom I worked took an interest in me and exposed me to the life of diplomats. Although I became convinced during those months I was interning that I did not want to join the Foreign Service, I appreciated the mentoring. I was especially impressed that Warren Christopher, then the deputy secretary of state, came to speak to us. Years later, as secretary of state, I always made it a point to engage the interns. "I tell people to be good to their interns," I would say to them. "You never know where they might end up."

With only a few weeks to go in my internship, a college friend called to say that Dr. Korbel was gravely ill and likely would not last through the night. I was stunned. I thought that he had been diagnosed with hepatitis, but apparently that was the secondary condition. He had liver disease and it had progressed very rapidly. His daughter, Madeleine, called to see if I could come home for the funeral. I declined, explaining that I had a big end-of-the-summer presentation to make to the assistant secretary. Madeleine said that she understood. I sent flowers but felt incredibly guilty for not having made the trip back to Denver. I still do.

chapter twenty-eight

Returning to Denver without Dr. Korbel to guide me was disorienting. In the immediate aftermath of his death, I lost focus for the better part of a year. I made little progress toward choosing a dissertation topic, let alone working on it. My dedication to my academic work diminished significantly, and I spent a lot of time either goofing off or playing tennis. Life was full of interesting diversions, but I was twenty-four, living at home, still teaching piano, and making little progress toward getting out of school. Every time I went to register for a new quarter, the registrar, who'd known me since my freshman days, would say, "Are you still here?"

Adding to my vague frustration was the difficulty I faced in being an adult child in my parents' house. For example, there was the expectation that I should account for my whereabouts. One evening I stayed out late—really late—with some friends. When I got home my parents were worried and furious. "Why didn't you at least call?" I responded that I was an adult and didn't have to call. But a few weeks later when my parents went to an anniversary party and didn't call me, not returning home until one in the morning, I understood their point. After that, we agreed to keep each other informed so that no one worried.

By the beginning of 1979, I was increasingly frustrated and so were my parents. My father asked pointedly when I planned to finish. But, as was typical of my parents, rather than criticize me, they asked if there was anything holding me back. I explained that I needed to find a way to improve my Russian and wanted to study in Moscow. The problem was that in the 1970s most of the exchange programs would not take students who were studying modern Soviet politics. I was a budding Soviet specialist who had never been to the Soviet Union. Somehow my parents came up with the money themselves to send me to the Soviet Union in July of that year. The idea was for me to attend a major political science conference and then work on my Russian at Moscow State University.

My first exposure to Moscow had an enduring impact on me. The first time I saw Red Square and the Kremlin I somehow knew that I had made the right decision in choosing to study the Soviet Union. While life was not easy—fresh food was hard to find and the rooms were basic at best—I learned so much. I loved riding the elaborate subways, exploring Moscow and Leningrad, and spending time with Russian students. My linguistic skills improved considerably as I moved from using the language in the classroom to using it in real life.

One incident illustrated the point. When my roommates

and I first arrived we found to our horror that our rooms were infested with roaches. I was deputized to go and tell our hall lady about the problem. I approached her gingerly and said in my best Russian, "Y *nas y'est klopi*," meaning "We have bugs." At least, that is what I thought I had said. But the word for "roach" is actually *tarakan*. I had unwittingly told the woman that we had lice. She recoiled, undoubtedly thinking that this was exactly what one could expect of Americans.

I came back from Moscow in the fall refreshed and ready to sprint to the finish line. For my dissertation I had decided to study civil-military relations in Eastern Europe, and chose to work on the case of Czechoslovakia. The Russian professor at Denver was Czech, and I convinced him to start a class in the Czech language. I talked five other students into joining me, though to this day I am puzzled as to why they agreed. Nonetheless, I learned Czech well enough to conduct research in it.

That fall I also applied for and received a coveted internship for the summer of 1980 at the RAND Corporation in Santa Monica, California, where I worked on research projects related to my interest in the Soviet Union's military alliance, the Warsaw Pact. The internship was a breakthrough—I was beginning to collect experience and meet some of the best-known security specialists in the country.

Throughout my life, however, something has always come along to shake things up just when I am feeling settled. Maybe this is the fate of a striver, someone always trying to be "twice as good," so that just good is never enough. The RAND internship had come on the heels of an even more fundamental turning point in my life: I became a Republican.

* * *

In the wake of the Soviet invasion of Afghanistan in December 1979, everyone was worried about growing tensions between the United States and the Soviet Union. I'd previously registered as a Democrat and voted for President Jimmy Carter in my first presidential election in 1976; I had this narrative in my head about reconciliation of the North and South and how he was going to be the first Southern president. Now I watched him say that he had learned more about the Soviet Union from this Afghanistan invasion than he had ever known. "Whom did you think you were dealing with?" I asked the television set. When Carter decided that the best response to the invasion was to boycott the Olympics, he lost me. I voted for Ronald Reagan in 1980, and a few years later I joined the Republican Party.

The security situation convinced the Ford Foundation that there was a need for people who were expert both in Soviet affairs and in hard-core, bombs-and-bullets security policy. I applied for the inelegantly named Dual Expertise Fellowship in Soviet Studies and International Security. When I received notice I'd won, there were four choices for where I could conduct my research: Harvard, UCLA, Columbia, and Stanford. I eliminated UCLA. I'd liked RAND but didn't really want to return to Southern California. I sent inquiries to the other three. Harvard didn't answer my letter. My colleagues there dispute this now, but trust me, I didn't get an answer. My father eliminated Columbia, saying that he didn't want me to live in such a dangerous neighborhood in New York. Fortunately, Stanford answered, and I was quick to accept the offer.

chapter twenty-nine

The news that I would be accepting the fellowship and leaving for Stanford in the fall of 1980 was greeted with a mixture of pride and sadness by my parents. Despite the fact that the Stanford fellowship was for only one year, Daddy sensed that I would never return to Denver, and that made him very sad.

It was also a time of uncertainty in my father's life. While Daddy was increasingly active and well regarded as a community leader, things were changing at the university. Chancellor Mitchell, who'd been Daddy's strong mentor and friend, had retired in the spring of 1978, and the new chancellor was not particularly close to my father. For the first time in my memory, Daddy felt professionally vulnerable. He sought out other employment opportunities, but no one wanted to hire a man in his late fifties.

Daddy's health was also a growing concern. Like many former athletes, my father had very bad knees, and as he got older he stopped exercising and gained weight. At the age of fifty-four he was diagnosed with both high blood pressure and diabetes. His father had died of a heart attack. Yet Daddy simply couldn't muster the willpower to lose weight. The two of us clashed regularly about his eating habits, but he just couldn't give up the fried food—pork chops, in particular—of his Southern upbringing.

Nonetheless, we both knew that I couldn't pass up an opportunity to go to Stanford. I decided to defer until the winter quarter, however. I took a part-time job in Denver in order to make a little more money before I left for the fellowship. I also wanted to give my parents—and, frankly, myself—a little more time to get used to the idea of a departure that might be permanent.

I called Stanford to tell the director of the arms control program, John Lewis, that I would come in January. John said that it would be no problem to defer but invited me out to Palo Alto for a November conference so that I could get acquainted with everyone.

When I arrived at Stanford, I was overwhelmed by its beauty and unnerved by its reputation. Stanford's 8,180 acres, set against the foothills of northern California, were once the farm of Senator Leland Stanford and his wife, Jane Lathrop Stanford. In 1885, the Stanfords donated the land for a university that would honor their only child, who'd died of typhoid fever at sixteen. The university is thus colloquially called "the Farm." It was a good regional university until the mid-1950s, when its reputation skyrocketed, particularly in the sciences and engineering. By 1980 it was an elite university whose only real peers resided in the Ivy League.

That first morning I walked from the Faculty Club, where I was staying, to Galvez House, where the arms control program was located. As I made my way along the long colonnade flanked with sandstone columns, I felt a level of insecurity that I'd never felt before and have never felt since. I'd been slowly climbing out of the obscurity of the University of Denver, but I couldn't quite believe that I was about to become a doctoral fellow at Stanford. A part of me wondered if the university had made a mistake.

Galvez House was a dumpy one-story sandstone building that had once been a dormitory for university laborers. The other fellows, including three women, greeted me. It seems that the Stanford arms control program had never had a woman fellow before 1980. Now it had four: Janne Nolan, Gloria Duffy, Cynthia Roberts, and me. There was a subtle competitiveness between us but also a sense of shared sisterhood as we talked about building careers in the male-dominated field of national security policy. Together with the assistant director, Chip Blacker, we'd form a tight bond. I knew that when I returned in the winter, I'd feel right at home.

The time until my departure for Palo Alto went by swiftly. I continued to work on my dissertation, trying to finish as much as I could before departing. There were also a lot of farewells to my friends. But as January approached, I could hardly wait to go.

Two days after the New Year, I came home one day to find Mother lying on the sofa, clearly in distress from horrendous stomach pains. She went up to bed, but in the middle of the night, my father came into my room and said that Mother's temperature had spiked to 103 degrees. He was going to take her to the emergency room. I didn't want to delay them and said that I'd meet him at the hospital.

Sitting in the waiting room, my father and I prayed. My mother was a cancer survivor, and both of us immediately worried that this illness might somehow be related. Those fears were reinforced when my mother's physician, Dr. Hamilton, came out to say that the imaging showed a large unidentifiable mass in her abdomen. "I don't know what it is," he said, "but I'm going to get it out. Now!"

"Dr. Hamilton, could it be related to her cancer?" I asked.

"I just don't know," he replied, and rushed off down the hall to prep my mom for surgery.

Waiting rooms outside of surgical units are, to my mind, the most unpleasant places on earth. You sit and read magazines, the substance of which you care nothing about and of which you remember nothing. My father and I sat together watching the hands move glacially on the black-rimmed clock on the wall.

Finally Dr. Hamilton came out. I could see the relief on his face immediately. Mother had suffered a burst appendix several days before. He explained that this was causing toxins to spread through her system, setting off a raging infection and thus the high temperature. The appendix had actually broken into two parts, resulting in the weird image that he'd seen on the ultrasound. "She'll be fine, but she is going to be pretty sick for a while," he said.

I was scheduled to leave for Palo Alto a few days later. Mother, still weak and very frail, insisted that I go. When I boarded the plane, she was out of intensive care but still very sick. It wasn't the way that I wanted to start my new life in Palo Alto. But each time I called, she sounded better. I was relieved when she was finally home, and I resolved to go back to Denver within a couple of months—just to see for myself.

chapter thirty

I settled into a studio apartment in the Alma Village Apartments in Palo Alto. It was about two miles from campus, alongside the Caltrain railroad tracks. The apartment complex overlooked a gas station that never seemed to have any customers, a strip mall with a Lucky's grocery store, a cleaners, and a Chinese restaurant whose kung pao chicken was of questionable origin. But the "Moon Palace," as one of my friends who also lived there nicknamed it, had a swimming pool, where at the age of twenty-five I finally learned to swim.

Boris, my cute little Oldsmobile Omega of Notre Dame days, had long since become unreliable, and, unable to afford a new ride, I gratefully accepted my parents' old car. Thus I drove to Stanford each day in a huge green Chevrolet Impala that my friends nicknamed "the football field."

Galvez House was a great place to work, and I made rapid progress toward finishing my dissertation, an accomplishment that had eluded me in Denver. "Dissertations don't write themselves," I tell my students now. It's a fact that I learned from the discipline of getting up every day and writing a few hours in the morning. I was the only morning person among the fellows and largely had the office to myself until about noon. Once Janne, Gloria, and Cindy arrived, I found that my productivity slowed as we engaged in hall conversation about everything from missile defense to movies. We went to dinner together a couple of times a week. And Janne and I would go shopping, one such trip to Saks resulting in the purchase of our first pair of Ferragamo shoes, which neither of us could afford but which we bought anyway. I also established a lifelong friendship with Chip and his partner, Louie Olave, who often invited us to their house for dinner and dancing to Louie's amped-up stereo. I loved Stanford.

That didn't mean that I'd overcome the insecurity associated with my rapid ascent from Denver to one of the world's best universities. It could be a bit intimidating to learn from prominent national policy makers. Though I began to feel comfortable in elite academia, I still had moments of doubt. For example, every fellow was required to prepare a seminar on his or her dissertation. While the exercise was intended to be a helpful step toward finishing the dissertation, it was actually a fairly nerve-wracking experience. Seated at the head of the table in the overcrowded conference room, I started out slowly, looking for any sign of approval as the presentation went along. About halfway through I saw a Japanese colonel who was visiting that day nodding vigorously in support of what I was saying. This fired me up. If my presentation on civil-military relations was meeting with the approval of this career military officer, I thought, I must be doing well. The affirmation fueled me through the rest of the presentation and the question-and-answer session that followed. When I finished I walked over to him, hoping to engage him about my topic. It was then that I learned he spoke no English.

A few weeks after my seminar, John Lewis, the program's director and one of the world's most eminent China scholars, called me into his office. John said that the Political Science Department had invited me to give a seminar for their faculty the following week. So the next week I repeated the presentation that I'd given at Galvez House for a somewhat smaller but far more skeptical audience. When I'd finished the presentation, the first question came from Heinz Eulau, the chair of the Political Science Department. Heinz believed that the study of politics was a science and any worthwhile project had to be quantifiable in some way. The kind of analytical/descriptive work that I did was not scientific enough for him. And he looked down on "area studies," which posited the uniqueness of, say, Russia, or the importance of the study of culture and language in China.

I knew Heinz's work and braced myself for what I expected to be a hostile question. He took his time, taking one more puff on his pipe before speaking. "How," he asked after what seemed like an eternity, "can any of what you have said be rigorous enough to have any theoretical value? You can't measure anything." I'd anticipated that line of attack. Going back to the work I'd done at Notre Dame, I explained that I could not quantify the relationship between Soviet power and the response of the Czech military but that I could ask

rigorously structured questions and examine alternative ex-
planations. I then proceeded to do so. Heinz cocked his head
to the side and his eyes twinkled—something that I later
learned to read as a signal of approval. The rest of the
question-and-answer session went smoothly.

A few days later, John called me in again. The Political
Science Department had an opening for a specialist in international political economy and Heinz wanted me to apply.

"But John, I do international security," I protested.

"That's okay. Just apply," he told me.

So I put together my resume and the one article that I
had written and sent it forward to the Department. The answer came back that they were looking for someone in political economy. Nonetheless, they'd been impressed with my
work and wanted to explore a three-year term appointment,
meaning that it could *not* lead to tenure (a status that may be
granted to a professor after a trial period of several years, and
which protects the faculty member from being dismissed for
no cause). In addition, I would serve as the assistant director
of the Arms Control Center; Chip would be promoted to associate director. I told John that I was interested and wanted
to talk to Heinz about it.

I walked across campus that sunny and warm April afternoon wondering if indeed I was about to join the Stanford faculty. "Could this really be happening?" I asked myself
out loud. But when I got to Heinz's office, he didn't offer me
the term appointment.

"Would you be interested in a tenure-line appointment?"
he asked.

At first I didn't think I'd heard him correctly. But he

proceeded to explain that the eminent Soviet expert Alexander Dallin and several other faculty members of the Political Science Department had been very impressed with my seminar and wanted to hire me. Usually they didn't do things this way, instead conducting an intensive search from among hundreds of candidates when there was a position open.

"You do understand that there would be nothing special done for you at the time of tenure," he went on. "You'll sink or swim just like everyone else. It won't matter how you got here. Only thirty percent of the people who come up for tenure get it. In fact, there is a review after three years, and it is likely that you won't make it through that."

"I see," I said. "That sounds fair—after three years you can see if you like me, and I can decide if I like you."

Heinz smiled. I don't think he had ever encountered anyone naïve enough about faculty hiring at an elite university to say something so dumb.

A few days later, I got a call from Stanford's affirmative action officer, asking if we could have lunch. We went to the faculty club and talked for a while. At the end of the conversation she said that she'd wanted to meet me because my case had been unusual. Usually she was in the position of pushing departments to hire minorities. If a department was willing to hire a minority professor, the university would provide half the money for the position. Even with that incentive, departments were reluctant. But this time the department had come to her. "How did this happen?" she asked. I told her the story, but I didn't really understand what was going on myself.

Years later, after having been on the other side of faculty hiring, especially as the provost of Stanford, I understood exactly what had happened. Stanford, in an effort to diversify its faculty, had made it possible to hire minorities without going through the normal processes. The Department of Political Science saw a young, black, female Soviet specialist and decided to make an affirmative action hire.

Contrary to what has sometimes been written about me, I was and still am a fierce defender of affirmative action of this kind. Why shouldn't universities use every means necessary to diversify their faculty? And frankly, any new assistant professor, no matter how promising, is a risk: some will succeed and some will not. The tenure process is a proving ground. A lot happens between hiring and judgment day.

I went home for Easter a few days after receiving the Stanford offer and talked it through with my parents. Sitting in the kitchen, my father and I at the table, my mother preparing dinner at the stove, I asked their advice. While I was thrilled that Stanford wanted me, I still had reservations about an academic career. I had several other job offers and was not sure what to do. Sitting in the kitchen, Daddy asked how much each job offered. Stanford was offering $21,000, about $5,000 less than the others. "Take the twenty-one thousand," he said.

I was surprised, not because he wanted me to take the lower salary but because I had assumed that he'd want me to stay in Denver. "Why?" I asked.

"It's Stanford," he answered.

I explained that the process had been irregular and asked what he thought of being hired under affirmative action.

"Don't worry about it," he said. "Their 'processes' have been excluding us for years. Just go and show them how good you are."

After Easter, I returned to Stanford and made an all-out effort to finish my dissertation, working seven or eight hours every day toward its completion. The reviews from my committee were positive. This was especially true of the evaluation I received from Michael Fry, by far the most difficult critic. He'd left the Denver deanship for the University of Southern California and suggested that I come down to Pasadena to go over his comments. After dinner at his home, he launched into his comments, but it was clear that he thought my work was nearly done.

That night I stayed at the Frys' home. As I lay in bed, a deep sense of satisfaction, almost wonder, came over me. I was indeed about to become a PhD, and I had landed a coveted job at Stanford. I said a little prayer of thanksgiving and drifted off to sleep.

chapter thirty-one

The August commencement at Denver University was really a cause for celebration. Both my high school and under-graduate graduations had been anticlimactic. Now, with the receipt of my PhD and the job offer at Stanford, my parents and I could acknowledge that all they had tried to do—even that premature stab at early education when I was three—had paid off. The night before the ceremonies, there was a large reception at the Phipps Mansion, a beautiful old white elephant that had been deeded to the university by one of Denver's most important families. At one point, the master of ceremonies read off a list of where the PhD students had been hired. When he read my name and said Stanford, there was an audible reaction of approval and surprise. My parents just beamed.

Several friends had traveled from out of town to attend commencement, and there were many more from Denver.

My parents held a big dinner afterward at our favorite restaurant. At the dinner, Daddy choked up when trying to make a toast. It took him a while to regain his composure and to say, "Your mother and I always knew that you were special. You are God's child." My parents had said this before to friends and family, and I always found it embarrassing.

I tried to deflect the comment by saying something like, "We're all children of God." But that commencement night Daddy wouldn't be deterred, repeating the phrase again and again. Finally, I just changed the subject to make a joke about the gifts that I'd been given.

"You all gave me household gifts," I said. It was true. I had gotten fancy candlesticks and linens as well as a beautiful set of silverware. "Maybe you thought this was a bridal shower," I joked.

I wasn't required to teach in my first quarter at Stanford. That's not unusual, since the university tries to give new assistant professors a chance to get their feet on the ground before taking on the Stanford student body. But I would be required to teach three courses after the first of the year. And unfortunately, graduate school doesn't really prepare students for teaching responsibilities. At best, an advanced graduate student will act as a teaching assistant to faculty a few times. The whole process of graduate education is geared toward compiling a research record. That is the basis on which elite universities hire assistant professors. In those days, no one even asked whether the job candidate could teach. Frankly, they still don't.

I sat down with Heinz to decide what three courses I

would teach. Obviously, it made sense to offer a course on civil-military relations, the topic of my dissertation. I said that I could also offer a course on Soviet policy in the Third World. But I had no earthly idea what else to propose. Heinz asked whether I could teach something called Elite Politics. I immediately said yes, though I didn't really know what one would do in such a class. Perhaps sensing my discomfort, Heinz said, "Let's co-teach the course in the spring." I felt as if I'd been delivered from certain doom, and readily agreed. I would teach civil-military relations in the winter. In the spring I would teach Soviet Policy in the Third World and co-teach Elite Politics with Heinz.

As winter quarter approached, I realized that my proposed course on civil-military relations had not been listed in the course catalogue. The irregular process by which I had been hired had somehow failed to trigger the normal mechanisms. An embarrassed Heinz said that the department would widely advertise my course. When January rolled around, six—yes, six—students had signed up for the course. Moreover, because the course was a late addition, all of the classrooms had already been booked. Thus, the morning of my first class at Stanford, I walked to the other side of campus and met my six students in the old chemistry building. The classroom even had one of those old sliding blackboards and a periodic table of the elements. I hadn't been in a room like that since Mrs. Sutter's chemistry class at St. Mary's Academy.

I was anxious at the outset of the class that January morning. Stanford students have a well-deserved reputation for showing young faculty who's smarter—and of course the students assume they are. The course met three times a week, and I was struggling, working late into the night to read and reread the material that I had assigned. I was just flat-out exhausted every day.

As the quarter progressed, I grew accustomed to life in the department. It wasn't always easy, since there were only two women, both of us junior faculty. It didn't help that Heinz often addressed the assembled faculty as "gentlemen." In time, I started to realize that I was a really good teacher. My first students gave me outstanding evaluations and when I taught the course the next year, its ranks swelled to fifty. By the third year, The Role of the Military in Politics was over-enrolled and I cut off admission at 120.

On balance, my first year was satisfying but very hard. In addition to teaching, you're expected to push ahead with your research agenda. Much to my surprise, Princeton University Press offered to publish my dissertation as a book. Princeton was the gold standard for university presses, and publishing a first book with them was a real coup.

During my first year, I made a point of getting to know key leaders at Stanford, many of whom acted as mentors to me. I've never subscribed to the idea that you have to have role models who look like you. If that were the case, there would be no firsts. My friend and former neighbor Sally Ride never would have been an astronaut if she had waited to see a female in that role. Sure, it's good to have female or minority role models. But the important thing is to have mentors who care about you, and they come in all colors. Thus, I made certain years later as an administrator that I always made time to see junior faculty who asked. And many did—including lots of white males.

There were dinners and parties almost monthly, and "sings" at John Lewis's house, where the assembled would croon old favorites such as the Depression-era anthem "Hallelujah, I'm a Bum." As odd as the social outings were, the people were really genuine and gave me a tight-knit community to which I could belong. And Stanford sports provided yet another touchstone. I bought season football tickets and enjoyed afternoons at the Stanford stadium, where future famed Broncos quarterback John Elway was then in his senior season. Season tickets for basketball followed.

I also reconnected with church life, though initially through the Baptists, not the Presbyterians. Frankly, with all the upheaval of the move I'd fallen away from the discipline of weekly church attendance. One Sunday morning (when I should have been in church) I was grocery shopping at Lucky's. A black man named Dale Hamel walked up to me in the spice aisle and began to talk. There just aren't that many black people in Palo Alto, so I was surprised to learn that he was buying food for a church picnic at Jerusalem Baptist Church, a long-standing black congregation. We chatted for a while, and then he asked, "Do you play the piano? We need someone to play the piano." I answered yes and within about a week began to play for the choir. Despite my marginal talent for gospel music, I served as the pianist at Jerusalem for about six months. But since the long arm of the Lord had reached all the way into the spice aisle at Lucky's, I resolved to find a good Presbyterian church and get back to weekly attendance. I soon joined Menlo Park Presbyterian Church, which has been my church home ever since. Stanford and California were turning out to be very good for me.

There were troubles back in Denver, however. Ironically, my mother, for whom Denver had never really been a comfortable fit, was doing quite well. Mother was teaching at Gove Middle School and was about to complete a master's degree at the University of Denver's Graduate School of International Studies, where I had done my PhD. The degree, through the Center for Teaching International Relations, prepared high school teachers to teach international subject matter. She loved the program, and the work brought her closer to my world.

For Daddy, though, life was turning sour. Sitting at my desk at Galvez House one fall morning in 1982, I received a call from him. He was obviously upset, saying that he'd been told that the university would no longer have a job for him after the end of the school year. He was particularly worried about the imminent loss of health insurance. We eventually worked it out so that he retired from the university, thereby retaining health coverage and his pension. But I was furious with the university. Many years later, when I was asked to accept the Evans Award for outstanding alumni, I did so only on the condition that my father be acknowledged too. To this day I'm a major supporter of the Graduate School of International Studies, which was renamed in honor of my advisor Dr. Korbel, but I don't feel close ties to the broader university.

Daddy's situation threw everything into a tailspin. The house that my parents had bought in 1979 had been a stretch for them financially on two salaries. Now they simply couldn't afford the mortgage. That spring I went back to Denver and helped Mother and Daddy find a small but very nice condo not far from where they'd lived. It broke my heart to see their furniture, particularly the grand piano, jammed into the small living room. Mother had always wanted a house of her own and had finally gotten it, only to have to sell it a few years later. We all pretended that it was better since I was no longer at home and they didn't really need the space. It was true that the old house was a lot to maintain, and Daddy was glad not to have to cope with the flight of stairs that made his knees ache. But losing the house was a bitter pill for Mother and a source of deep embarrassment for my dad. For me it was more evidence that my parents' investment in me—skating, piano, St. Mary's Academy—had cost them dearly in terms of their own financial security.

Eventually my parents adjusted to their new life. Mother continued to teach, carrying most of the financial burden. My father was able to piece together consulting work and became very active with a nonprofit that counseled troubled young men and helped them find work. He loved it, but it paid him almost nothing. Daddy kept looking for new employment, but nothing materialized. Yet he maintained his dignity and sense of humor.

I tried to help my parents financially when I could. They visited me in California each Thanksgiving between 1982 and 1984. I paid their way, calling it their early Christmas present so as not to embarrass them. Occasionally, if I received a little extra income from a speech or an honorarium for an article, I'd just pay a bill for them without saying so.

But I too was under some financial strain, since I'd decided to buy my first house in the fall of 1982. With my Princeton book contract in hand, I was pretty sure that I would make it through the three-year review and be reappointed to the faculty. I decided to take the home-ownership plunge. Stanford offered very generous assistance to young professors who wanted to buy in the insane housing market of northern California. When I needed to dip into my grandfather's small trust to help with the down payment, I called Aunt Theresa, who was thrilled that I was doing the responsible thing and buying a house.

"How much does it cost?" she asked.

"A hundred and twenty-four thousand dollars," I answered.

"Don't you think that's a little above your means?" she huffed. Aunt Theresa was by this time living in Edwardsville, Illinois, and I am sure that her five-bedroom house was worth about half of what the two-bedroom, one-bath condo on the Stanford campus was about to cost me.

Fortunately, my father convinced her that it was a legitimate purchase, and I bought 74 Pearce Mitchell. I loved my little place, even though I could stand in the living room and see the entire condo. For several months I had to put my toothpaste purchases on my credit card, but in the long run the investment paid off.

Over the next few years I continued to do well at Stanford. My first book, *Uncertain Allegiance: The Soviet Union and the Czechoslovak Army*, was published. I was so happy to be able to give my mother the first advance copy as a Christmas present.

Toward the end of the 1984–85 school year, I received a call from the Stanford president's office letting me know that I would receive the Gores Award for Excellence in Teaching, the university's highest honor. The award would be bestowed at commencement, and the university would pay for my parents to come if they wanted. I waited until I knew they would both be home and called with the news. Though I couldn't see them, I knew that they were both crying. It was a thrilling moment for the three of us. Weeks later they attended the commencement ceremony, held under bright blue skies at the Stanford baseball stadium. It was one of our happiest days together.

chapter thirty-two

I started 1985 with growing confidence in the direction of
my career. Many young faculty are still trying to find a pub-
lisher for their initial book at the time of the third-year review. I was ahead of the game, having already published my
first book and being well on the way to designing a second research project. I was granted a sabbatical and applied for and
received a prestigious National Fellowship from the Hoover
Institution. I was particularly pleased that I could take my
sabbatical just a few paces across campus and did not have to
move. Feeling quite comfortable, professionally and even—
thanks to a couple of raises—financially, I bought a car with
my own money: a little rocket ship of a Buick that I named
Misha, the Russian nickname for the Soviet Union's leader
at the time, Mikhail Gorbachev. I thought I deserved a little
break, and for the first time in three years, I decided to go
home for Easter. ·

A day or so into my visit, I was watching television in the den when my mother came in with obvious bruises on her arm and leg.

"What happened?" I asked.

"I fell down the basement stairs on the way to do the laundry," she answered. "I'm getting clumsy in my old age. This is the second time this month!"

I didn't think much about it, assuming that she had just been careless. She also had a penchant for wearing high heels even when doing chores around the house. Maybe that was the explanation. I returned to Palo Alto after a lovely Easter and finished the quarter, planning to visit again sometime in the summer.

A few days before the Fourth of July, though, my father called. His usually strong voice was shaking. "I think I need to take your mother to the doctor," he said. "She keeps falling, and she seems really forgetful. The other day she asked our neighbor about a friend of ours from Alabama who's been dead for ten years."

July 5 was one of the darkest days of my life. Daddy called to say that Dr. Hamilton had taken an X-ray and there was a large mass on Mother's brain. The doctors were sure that it was inoperable and cancerous. Ever since Mother's breast cancer diagnosis, I'd feared this moment. Mother had done remarkably well for a long time. True, there had been a scare the year before when she'd required surgery to remove a small tumor on her lung. But she'd undergone follow-up chemotherapy during the summer of 1984 and had tolerated it well. She'd returned to work in the fall, and though I worried that the cancer, having returned once, might do so again, I'd buried that thought deep in my subconscious. But now I was faced with the worst possible news.

Mother got on the phone. "I've got this little thing in my head," she said. "It's not in such a bad place."

"Yes, Mother, but I want to come home for a little while," I said.

"Okay, but don't hurry," she replied.

When I got to Denver my father picked me up at the airport. We went directly to the hospital, where Mother was undergoing more tests. The room was pretty dimly lit, but Mother was remarkably upbeat. We talked for a while, and I didn't notice any of the mental deterioration of which my father had spoken. But the conversation with Dr. Hamilton couldn't have been clearer. When I asked how long she had, he said, "I've seen some people make it a year. But it won't be longer than that. I'm so sorry."

The doctors prescribed a treatment regimen for her. They were certain that surgery wasn't an option but believed tumor-shrinking radiation and medication could prolong her life. Every day I'd accompany Mother to the hospital, where she would undergo treatment. The effects were pretty devastating. Her once-beautiful hair began to fall out. She'd also lost some of her hair during the previous treatments in 1984, and we had actually had a little fun finding a wig that she loved wearing. But this was different. This time she was left with almost no hair. I was absolutely crushed when I saw her sitting on the bed holding a large clump of her hair in her hand and crying.

The four weeks in Denver were the hardest of my life. Mother's mental capacity was clearly diminished. One day I saw her sitting at the piano. She couldn't remember how to play. Yet when I sat down next to her on the bench and began to move her hands toward certain keys, she started to play—a few notes at first, and then miraculously a song, and then another and another. "I can play," she proclaimed. When she started to play "The Lord Knows How Much You Can Bear," I said to myself, *Mommy, I hope so*, and left the room in tears.

Daddy and I didn't really talk very much about what was happening. Life revolved around trying to make Mother comfortable. We went about the daily routine, even going out to brunch for her sixty-first birthday on July 21. As Daddy tried to raise his glass and say "Many happy returns," he finally broke down. Mother looked confused, not sad. It suggested to me that she didn't fully comprehend that she was dying.

I returned to Palo Alto at the end of July when my mother's sisters, Gee and Mattie, came out to be with her. I planned to teach my scheduled two-week alumni summer school session, go to a conference at Cornell, and then return to Denver in the middle of August.

Though I knew that she was gravely ill, I realize now that I just didn't let myself believe that I was losing my mother. Somehow I kept expecting a miracle, or perhaps I was just putting the awful truth out of my mind. But one day I was sitting at my desk at Galvez House when Herb Abrams stopped by. He was a world-renowned radiologist who was working at the center studying the potential effects of nuclear war. Herb had heard about Mother and wanted to offer his support. I think he was taken aback by my optimistic assessment of my mother's chances. "They say it's not the worst kind of brain tumor," I told him.

"Well, you make sure to spend time at home with her now. Don't wait," he replied.

The last session of the summer course I taught at Stanford was on Saturday, August 18. I had planned to leave the next day and stop in Denver overnight on my way to Cornell, just to check on Mother. After the two-day conference in Ithaca, where I would give a paper, I intended to return to Denver and stay for several weeks. There would be no pressure to return to Stanford early in the fall since I was beginning the Hoover sabbatical. And I was pleased that the summer teaching and the conference paper were yielding additional income. I intended to use the money to help my parents, since my mother would no longer be able to teach.

Mother had not been doing very well that weekend. I had talked to her several times that Saturday and she seemed weak, unable to finish a full sentence without running out of breath.

"Why don't you take her to the hospital?" I asked my father.

"She doesn't want to go," he said.

I called Saturday night before going to bed. "She's a bit better," Daddy said.

Hours later the phone rang, jerking me out of a very deep sleep. "Ann isn't breathing," Daddy said.

"What?" I asked, still not fully awake.

"I've called the ambulance because your mother isn't breathing," he said, clearly frightened but relatively calm.

217

"Call me when you get to the hospital," I said. I just lay in the dark and prayed. Over and over, I asked God not to take my mother.

Daddy called back less than an hour later. "She's gone," he said.

"I'll be there first thing in the morning," I told him.

"No need to hurry. She belongs to the ages now," he replied.

After I hung up the phone it occurred to me that Daddy must have been alone at the hospital. I called a friend of my mother's, who agreed to meet my father at the hospital. I didn't want to be alone either, so I called my dearest friend, Chip Blacker. When he answered the phone, I simply said, "Mother's dead, Chip. Can you come over?" He did so, sleeping on the sofa while I tried to go back to sleep for a few hours. I already had reservations to Denver the next morning.

Chip drove me to the airport, and I boarded the United Airlines plane for what seemed like the longest flight of my life. Going to my seat, I ran into a former student.

"Hi, are you going home to Denver for a visit?" she asked, knowing nothing of my mother's death.

"My mother died last night," I said. Then, to reinforce the point more for myself than for her, I said, "My mother's gone."

A friend picked me up at the airport and drove me to my parents' house. My father greeted me at the door and we hugged each other, tears flowing gently. His first words surprised me. "She was such a fighter. She fought to stay with us. She fought so hard," he said. He was right. Ever since her first bout with cancer Mother had refused to let her own circumstances intrude on our family's life. Because she'd been so tough and unyielding to her disease, sometimes even making light of it, we had been able to get on with our lives.

Daddy continued pouring out his thoughts, saying that he already missed her but that he had thanked God for answering his prayer.

"What prayer?" I said, somewhat puzzled.

"The one that asked him not to leave me alone with a fifteen-year-old girl," he replied.

I was hurting then more than I ever had, but I too felt just a touch of gratitude that my mother had died when I was thirty, not fifteen. She'd seen me grow into a successful adult. I was so grateful that she'd held my first book, attended the teaching awards ceremony, and shared with my father a glimpse of how well I would do at Stanford.

Still, I was so incredibly sad. I went into my parents' bedroom and sat on the side of the bed. There I looked around a room filled with my mother's belongings: her jewelry box, family photos, and the heavy mahogany furniture that had been her pride and joy since I was a child. And then something happened. I felt my mother's spirit release, breaking its bonds with earth. There was the unmistakable sensation of someone or something leaving the room. I had not made it home before she died. Had she in some sense waited? This was a mystical moment that I have never been able to adequately describe. Yet I suddenly felt at peace. The Apostle Paul called it "the peace that passeth all understanding." I got down on my knees and prayed that God would take care of Mother's eternal soul.

Daddy and I planned a very small funeral, not making a newspaper announcement of her death until the day after the service. My mother did not have many close friends outside of her family, and a public funeral just seemed wrong. About fifty friends and family—her brothers and sisters and my cousins—gathered at Montview Boulevard Presbyterian Church and then at the cemetery. We laid her to rest elegantly dressed in a gray and black dress and very high black heels. Even after all that she had been through, she still looked very beautiful. It wasn't too hard to picture the long-ago image of the pretty young teacher. The thought crossed my mind briefly that I should have dressed her in red.

chapter thirty-three

It is often said that the hardest days after the loss of a loved one are when all of the mourners leave and you're truly alone. Mother was buried on a Wednesday, and the last family member, my cousin Denise, left that Sunday. My father and I went back to the apartment and there was truly nothing to do. We tried watching television but finally decided to go out to dinner. The two of us had never been at a loss for words, but now we were. Daddy kept ordering vodka. I snapped at him that he had had enough. "I need you to be with me," I blurted out. He didn't drink any more. We sat in silence.

The next day we took care of a number of business matters, primarily insurance and financial tasks. Daddy said that he'd like to visit his mother and sister in Illinois. My eighty-eight-year-old grandmother was pretty frail and Daddy had discouraged her from attending the funeral. The trip to Illinois turned out to be good for him, but I worried about returning to Stanford and leaving him alone. I suggested that we go directly from Illinois to Palo Alto, where he could spend a couple of weeks with me. My friend Randy picked us up at the airport, and years later she'd tell me that she was worried for Daddy's survival when she saw him. "He was as broken as any person I had ever seen," she said.

One evening during Daddy's stay, I arranged a little dinner at my house. Harold Boyd, a black colleague from Stanford, invited a few people closer to my dad's age. Daddy had a great time that evening and in his subsequent meetings at the university, brainstorming with the director of Stanford's Public Service Center about programs to involve the university in the broader community.

After a couple of weeks, Daddy said that it was time for him to return to Denver. He told me he really liked Palo Alto and might consider moving but wanted to think about it. I encouraged him to do so, telling him that we only had each other and should be together. I didn't push, figuring he needed time to decide. So I put him on the plane in early September, though I worried constantly about him.

I was having a rough time too. I threw myself into my work at Hoover, but the sadness was sometimes overwhelming. I had many friends and found plenty to do, but I felt incredibly empty. Deep despair could be triggered by seemingly innocuous events. One evening in the checkout line at the grocery store, I saw a woman of about seventy. She was wearing comfortable old-lady shoes. *My mother will never grow old,* I thought. I left my groceries on the counter and ran to my car, where I sobbed uncontrollably until the feeling passed.

The first weekend in October, Randy suggested that we

take a football trip. I was by this time a rabid fan of the Cincinnati Bengals (the Browns had folded for a time), and Randy loved the New York Giants. The two teams were playing in Cincinnati, where she had family and a place to stay, so we decided to make the trip.

I got up that Sunday morning in Cincinnati and called my dad to check on him. I noticed that he sounded more cheerful than he had in many weeks.

"Daddy, what are you doing?" I asked him.

"I'm packing up," he said. "The movers will be here tomorrow. I'll be in Palo Alto on Wednesday."

Daddy had arranged a visiting fellowship through the university's Public Service Center and rented an apartment. I later learned that he was already in touch with Harold Boyd from dinner and a new friend, Lois Powell. Harold was a little surprised to find that my father hadn't told me he was moving. So was I, but I couldn't have been happier. I wanted to be with my dad. I was really pleased that he wanted to be with me too.

Within a few weeks, Daddy had settled in. In addition to diving into his work at the Public Service Center, he once again befriended and began to counsel student athletes. My father was making friends as rapidly as he always had. His little apartment, stuffed with the family furniture, became a gathering place for all kinds of people—especially middle-aged ladies who brought him food. Daddy would, in turn, invite them out to dinner or buy them Valentine's Day candy. After about six months he asked me, "Do you think I'm dating?" It was so cute. I answered that yes, I thought he was, and that I was very happy about it. He beamed and continued to ask

223

the ladies out—several of them. Yet he kept a crocheted plaque above the refrigerator that said "Angelena's Kitchen."

We still had our moments of great sadness, the most wrenching coming the first Christmas Day after Mother's death. The holiday season had been tolerable. We engaged in many of the Christmas traditions we always had, decorating both my house and his and shopping for family presents. But on Christmas morning when we lit the last Advent candle the emptiness was overwhelming. We'd received an invitation from my senior faculty colleague Jan Triska to join his family for dinner. I'd declined, thinking that Daddy and I would want to be alone. But as we sat in silence after dinner, I decided that we had to get out of the house. I called Jan and we went to his home for dessert. I have been forever grateful to the Triska family for the kindness of that invitation and the respite it provided on that difficult day.

Ultimately, I decided that Daddy was adjusting very well, so I felt freer to travel and accepted a three-week visiting professorship at the National Defense Academy of Japan, in Yokosuka. I had never been to Japan, and I have to admit that it was a somewhat hard place to be under the circumstances. The academy, their West Point, had never had a woman teach there. In fact, I don't think they had ever had a woman on the school grounds before I came. One clue was the absence of a ladies' room. The school solved the problem by making one of the men's rooms off-limits to everyone else but me. I never knew exactly what the huge sign on the door said, but it had a few too many characters to simply say "Do Not Enter." Later I would be pleased to learn that the academy admitted its first female cadet in 1992.

I also had a hard time adjusting to the rigid hierarchy. All military academies are hierarchical, but in Japan this is exacerbated by cultural customs. Somehow I could never learn to bow at exactly the right level. One day my host professor told me that I was bowing too low, requiring the cadets to try to go lower. The next day I wasn't bowing low enough. The language, which is also hierarchical, made it difficult to find an appropriate greeting in a case where a female of higher status addresses a male of lower standing. When one of my host professors invited me to his home for dinner and his wife served us but ate in the kitchen, I was just appalled. In general, I found the whole experience stultifying and looked forward to returning to my tiny hotel room every day.

I've always said that I love sports so much that I'll watch anything with a score at the end. In Japan that meant watching the Grand Sumo Wrestling Tournament. I actually came to like it, giving the wrestlers nicknames like Fred and Toby since I couldn't understand what was being said. To this day, I still like to watch sumo wrestling.

At the end of my trip, one of the professors told me that I'd been extremely successful in my teaching. "More important," he said in heavily accented English, "it shows the Japanese that not all black people are stupid." I knew that he meant it as a compliment, so I thanked him for his kindness. Fortunately, I've made many subsequent trips to an evolving Japan that have wiped away some of those early negative memories. I am happy to say that I'm now quite fond of the country, which has changed a lot in twenty-five years.

chapter thirty-four

In 1985 I had applied for both the Hoover fellowship and a fellowship from the Council on Foreign Relations. I was awarded both but asked the Council if I could defer for a year. The Council on Foreign Relations is a think tank that includes among its members all major American figures in international politics. Founded in 1921 and located in New York, it is arguably the most prestigious organization in the field.

The Council's International Affairs Fellowship is thus highly coveted. Young faculty and other midcareer professionals who are awarded the fellowship are given a yearlong appointment working for the federal government. I was offered positions in the National Security Council (NSC), the State Department, and the Pentagon. I wanted to work for the Joint Chiefs of Staff, reasoning that I might have other opportunities to work in civilian agencies but would find it difficult to land on a military staff again. Thanks in part to a Stanford colleague's successful tenure with the Joint Chiefs the year before, the military agreed to take me on. I told my colleague that they had gotten used to having a civilian around thanks to him; now we would see whether they were ready for a civilian black woman.

Stanford readily granted me a second year of sabbatical, though a few faculty friends wondered if leaving during the year when I would be considered for tenure was really wise. "Out of sight," one said, "out of mind."

For my part, I was more concerned about leaving my father yet again. He had lived in Palo Alto for ten months, and I'd been gone for three of them. I asked him to meet me for dinner at a local restaurant and started to talk about why it was so important for me to work for the Joint Chiefs. Then I just stopped and said, "Do you mind if I move to Washington for a year?"

"No," he replied, and then went on to ask if I could afford it financially. It was clear from his demeanor that he really didn't mind. He wanted me to go.

As it turned out, my year with the Joint Chiefs of Staff was one of the best of my life. I worked for the Nuclear and Chemical Division, which analyzed situations in which the United States would use its nuclear forces. As a Soviet specialist, I helped to develop guidance for the type of war that everyone thought unthinkable. As difficult as it was to contemplate such a scenario, this particular unit had to plan for it anyway. This led to black humor like the bottle of champagne that the division chief stashed in his drawer in the event of pending nuclear annihilation. When the missiles were on their way to Moscow and Moscow's were on their way to Washington, the plan was to pop the cork and kiss your "expletive" goodbye.

I loved working with these officers, who all held the rank of lieutenant colonel or naval commander. They were dedicated, smart, and relegated temporarily to office duty in the Pentagon: I could tell they all looked forward anxiously to the day when they could leave Washington and go command a ship or an air wing.

Truthfully, my officemates didn't know quite what to make of me when I arrived in the summer of 1986. On the first day, they informed me that it was the responsibility of the rookie to make the coffee. They probably thought I'd make a fuss or maybe even claim gender discrimination. I just made the coffee—really, really strong. I was never asked to make the coffee again. (It helped, too, that I won the first football pool of the year.)

It was also during this time that I first met General Colin Powell, then the deputy national security advisor. My meeting with him in his corner office in the West Wing of the White House was the start of our friendship. And by meeting with me, Colin had sent an important message throughout Washington that I was someone to keep an eye on. I never forgot that act of mentorship and kindness.

My time in Washington was interrupted in the fall by a health crisis of my own. One evening, while riding the metro from the Pentagon to my Van Ness Street apartment, I started to experience excruciating stomach pains. At first I chalked it up to stomach flu, but it simply got worse as the week went on. Fearing appendicitis, I took the next day off from work and went to a doctor. After a few questions and an exam, he told me it was likely that I had uterine fibroids— a nasty condition that can afflict as many as 80 percent of women. He arranged a consult with an obstetrician-gynecologist, who recommended that I have a hysterectomy.

This was terrible news. In the back of my mind I had always assumed that I would get married and have kids. I wanted to find that special man because I had been inspired by the wonderful example my parents had provided through their marriage. I was not at all concerned that marriage might hold me back professionally. Again, both of my parents had managed careers and family life quite well. But as I told (and still tell) my friends, you don't get married in the abstract; you have to want to marry a particular person. And frankly, I'd always hoped to marry within my race. If the right man does not come along, it is better to enjoy a fulfilling and happy life as a single person. But in 1986, at the age of thirty, the prospect of not even having the *option* to have kids was devastating.

That night, I called my ob-gyn back in Palo Alto and asked whether there were other approaches. She suggested that I come back and see a young doctor who was doing pioneering work in alternatives for women with my condition. I called the physician, who said that he couldn't be certain until he examined me, but he was having great success with myomectomy, which removed the fibroids and left the uterus intact. I immediately felt better and more in control of the situation. The next day, I informed my division chief that I needed to go home for a few weeks. It was just after Thanksgiving. I told him that I would likely return in January.

My father met me at the airport two days later. At his apartment I calmly went through the diagnosis that I had been given.

"Are they ever malignant?" Daddy asked.

"Only in about one percent of the cases," I said, relating what I had been told.

"I'm sure you will be all right," he said. I thought he was correct, but I was nonetheless very apprehensive: one percent seems a lot bigger when you are the daughter of a breast cancer victim. But a couple of nights before the surgery, I had a dream about my mother in which she affirmed that everything would indeed be all right. I'd never before had a premonition and have never had one since.

Several days later I had the surgery, which took more than seven hours. When I woke up in my room, I heard the doctor say that everything had gone fine. I looked around and saw my father and one or two friends, including John Lewis, who was smiling broadly. In my semidrugged state he looked a bit like one of those distorted faces in a horror movie. I closed my eyes and went back to sleep.

Though the surgery had been successful, the recovery was difficult. My digestive system shut down, which required that I undergo an extremely uncomfortable procedure to insert a tube through my nose and down my throat. After enduring two days of this, I called for my doctor. "If you don't remove this thing, I'm going to die," I told him. Fortunately, I got better and he decided to remove the tube—a little prematurely. He told me he was worried that I was so strong-willed I might die just to spite him.

All of this medical drama had been extremely wearing on my father. He practically lived at the hospital for that entire week. Finally on Friday, seven days after I'd had the surgery, I told him to go home and get some rest. I was to be discharged on Saturday and was feeling just fine. Shortly after Daddy left, the doctor came in and said that I could go home that night instead. Because I had rented my Stanford condo to another faculty member when I left for Washington, I went back to Daddy's apartment to recuperate.

At about three in the morning Daddy came in and woke me up. "Something isn't right with me," he said. "I've called 911."

Still groggy from pain medication, I got up and went into the living room, where Daddy had been sleeping on the pull-out sofa. He had thrown up, and he told me he was experiencing pain in his chest. An ambulance arrived moments later and rushed him to the hospital. I got dressed and called a friend, who took me there about thirty minutes later.

A young resident met me in the emergency room when I arrived at the Stanford Medical Center. He said Daddy was undergoing some tests and that he'd get back to me when he knew what had happened. After what seemed like an eternity, the doctor emerged to say that Daddy had indeed suffered what he described as a major heart attack. "The next twenty four hours are crucial," he said.

I called my friend Randy, who came over immediately and sat with me for the rest of the night. Finally they let me see Daddy, who was weak but in surprisingly good spirits. "This is a wake-up call," he said. "I've been tempting fate for a long time." I was relieved to see him talking and upbeat, but I was still very worried that I was going to lose him. I told Randy that I couldn't bear to lose my father just over a year after Mother's death.

Daddy had lost considerable heart function and would from then on suffer from congestive heart failure. Given that he also had diabetes and high blood pressure, his long-term prospects were not very good. But at least he was alive. He'd tempted fate, but at least for the time being, he'd won.

After the first of the year, I returned to Washington and resumed working for the Joint Chiefs. I felt more and more integrated into the daily life of the office, taking on my share of assignments, ranging from exciting ones to the more routine. One highlight was the opportunity to do a presentation in "the Tank," assessing President Reagan's idea of a world without ballistic missiles for the chairman and the Joint Chiefs. Although it's little more than a large conference room, the Tank carries a certain mystique in the military since it's the place where all-important decisions are made. I was so excited that I quite literally forgot to be nervous until the presentation was over. Frankly, it's not unusual for me to put the consequences of failure out of my mind until an event has finished. After my presentation in the Tank, I woke up in the middle of the night. *It was risky for you to come here and work for the military,* I thought. *This could have really backfired.* Then I went back to sleep.

A few days after the presentation, I received a phone call from the chair of the Political Science Department back at Stanford.

"The department has voted to recommend you for tenure," one of my colleagues, Steve Krasner, told me.

"Oh. I thought the vote was next week," I said clumsily and without a sense of how ungrateful that must have sounded.

Fortunately, Steve is an easygoing guy. "No, it was this week," he said, chuckling slightly.

Stanford's dean of the School of Humanities and Sciences, the university provost, and the Advisory Board (an elected body of seven senior faculty) still had to approve the department's recommendation, but I knew that they rarely overturned such decisions. I was pretty sure that I was about to receive tenure at Stanford. I called my father and my friend Chip. The truth is that I had been so busy preparing for my opportunity in the Tank that I'd forgotten all about the departmental vote. For that I was grateful; it turns out that it's far better to be out of sight during that awkward time when your colleagues are deciding your future.

The remainder of my time in Washington seemed to fly by. In addition to my work at the Pentagon, I was tapped in the spring of 1987 to do national television commentary for the first time. Out of the blue one day, the office secretary passed through a call from ABC News anchor Peter Jennings. I was a little stunned when this famous newsman said he'd like to meet for lunch. They were looking for "fresh faces," he said, and Bob Legvold, professor of Soviet studies at Columbia and an ABC News consultant, had recommended me.

Peter and I met, and after getting permission from my boss at the Joint Chiefs, I agreed to do some on-air commentary concerning U.S.-Soviet relations. This gave me my first national exposure and invaluable media experience. It also gave me a lifelong and dear friend in the late Peter Jennings.

I returned to Palo Alto in September 1987 and took up the duties of a tenured associate professor. I started new research activities that drew on my experiences in Washington and began taking new graduate students. I also took on some administrative duties, such as overseeing the graduate student admissions process for the Political Science Department. I even served on the search committee to select a new football coach for Stanford. It was great fun, and I especially enjoyed surprising the candidates with detailed questions about what kind of offense they'd run. Even the candidate who called me "sweetie" during the interview process was impressed that I knew Stanford was not an option offense team. (By the way, he didn't get the job.)

chapter thirty-five

I was pleased to see that Daddy had done very well in Palo Alto during my time in Washington. He'd made many friends and was active both with the university's Public Service Center and with the Stanford Department of Athletics. We settled into a nice pattern of getting together two or three times a week. Though we spoke by phone every day, we led separate and fulfilling lives.

By the start of 1988, the presidential campaign was heating up. George Herbert Walker Bush, the sitting vice president under Ronald Reagan, was the front-runner to become the Republican standard-bearer. I hadn't met Vice President Bush, but I did know his principal foreign policy advisor, General Brent Scowcroft. Brent was one of the wise men of the foreign policy establishment, having served Gerald Ford as national security advisor.

When Bush won the presidential election, Brent called

and asked me to join him at the National Security Council. Jim Baker also invited me to join him at the State Department as deputy director of policy planning, helping to oversee the department's internal think tank on strategic issues in foreign affairs. Then Senator Bill Cohen, whom I had gotten to know during my time with the Joint Chiefs, also called me—during the Super Bowl, no less—on behalf of the designee for defense secretary, John Tower, to offer me a job in the Pentagon. After a brief trip to Washington to check out the prospects, I settled on the job of director of Soviet and East European studies at the NSC. I decided that while the other jobs were interesting, there was nothing like being a member of the White House staff.

When I told Daddy that I wanted to take the job, he was not surprised. "You're going again!" he exclaimed, smiling broadly to let me know that it was fine with him. Stanford was quite surprised, since I would be taking my third leave of absence in four years. Nonetheless, the university approved an unpaid leave, and I headed to Washington.

I quickly learned that work at the National Security Council is hard and not very glamorous. Generally, NSC staffers write memoranda to prepare the President for phone calls and meetings, take notes to create a permanent record, coordinate with other government agencies to keep them on track with the administration's priorities, and just take care of whatever the President needs to do his job, whether it's whispering facts in his ear or photocopying his papers. In the past, though, the NSC staff had sometimes gotten too involved in carrying out the nation's foreign policy. The

Iran-Contra affair in the mid-1980s had been one such case, in which the NSC staff had secretly cooked up a plan to divert funds from covert Iranian arms sales to the Nicaraguan resistance (the Contras)—apparently without the knowledge of the secretary of state, let alone the Congress. The fallout was disastrous; the affair almost brought down the Reagan presidency. But Brent Scowcroft was a stickler for keeping the NSC staff in its proper place.

At the NSC, the hours are long, there is little tolerance for mistakes, and one must pay close attention to details. Sometimes the work has very little to do with serious policy making. My first task, only two days after I arrived in Washington, was to deal with a minor crisis involving the Soviet Union. It seems that a bakery cooperative somewhere in the USSR had sent a huge, several-hundred-pound cake congratulating President Bush on his election. By the time the cake arrived, it had crumbled into pieces, and a number of vermin had had their way with it. I went down to inspect the gift and suggested that we dispose of it—but only after taking a picture of the cake in a part of the White House that would be easily recognizable. We could then send the picture to the wonderful Soviet citizens who'd been so thoughtful.

I settled into my new job and life in Washington. Each morning I arrived at the White House at six-thirty and rarely left the office before nine at night. I found the work demanding, and I sometimes wondered if I'd make the cut. The NSC was known as a place where the weeding-out process was pretty severe: it wasn't uncommon to have a colleague with whom you were working on Monday disappear by Friday. No one ever asked what happened, but it was assumed that he or she had made an unforgivable mistake that embarrassed the White House or, even more unforgivably, the President.

I also knew that Brent preferred to have the NSC staff remain relatively anonymous and out of the spotlight. Brent set the standard as the most important man in Washington whom few Americans could identify in a photo lineup. But there was great media interest in me. When the *Washington Post* wanted to do a profile on the new Soviet specialist, a black woman professor from Stanford, I asked permission from Brent, who agreed I should do it. The morning the profile appeared, I was stunned to see a long, eye-catching article with a gigantic picture of me reading *Pravda*, a Soviet newspaper. It wasn't exactly the anonymity that was expected of the President's staff, and I was relieved when Brent called to say that he thought the article was terrific. Still, as my wonderful friend Vernon Jordan, the civil rights leader and venerable Washington lawyer, once warned me, Washington loved to create celebrities and then tear them down, and I resolved not to let celebrity status undermine my effectiveness. I don't know why I worried—I never had time to attend the cocktail parties and dinners that came with a high profile anyway.

Office and Washington politics aside, there were times that reminded me why I had chosen the White House over other, more senior jobs in the administration. The first such experience came when Brent called late on a wintry Friday afternoon in February. The President wanted to invite a group of Soviet specialists to his home in Kennebunkport, Maine, on Sunday to discuss the unfolding changes in

Moscow. At first I despaired at having to round up a group of academics so late on a Friday. I quickly learned, though, that when the White House calls, assistants and spouses manage to find people. So that Sunday, I met five other Soviet specialists at the airport in Portland, Maine. We made our way along the icy roads to Walker's Point, where we briefed the President in the bedroom—the only room at the time that had heat.

My first face-to-face encounter with the President was wonderful. He was kind and thanked me profusely for everything that I'd done. "You're so good to agree to leave California and help me out," he said. *Is he kidding?* I thought. *He's the President.* But I learned that day, and would see throughout my time with him, that this wasn't false modesty: George H. W. Bush is simply one of the nicest and most self-effacing people that I've ever met. He taught me so much about leading people. Countless times he would send a congratulatory note to a foreign leader for a seemingly innocuous achievement. I came to understand that he was building a relationship, which would serve him well when he needed to ask that leader to do something hard. Even I frequently received a thank-you note from the President for a job well done, and this kindness and courtesy made it a joy to work with him. Most important, his natural geniality served American diplomacy well when he was faced with revolutionary changes in world politics.

Because so much was unfolding in the Soviet Union and Eastern Europe, I began to see the President quite often. Just a few days after Kennebunkport, I was asked to meet with the U.S. ambassador to the Soviet Union and the President

in the Oval Office. I was overjoyed—and overwhelmed—
by simply being there. As I sat in the pale yellow room with
the sun streaming through the French doors, I suddenly realized that we were two-thirds of the way through the meeting and I hadn't taken a single note. This snapped me out of
my Condi-in-Wonderland moment. I went back to my office
and tried to re-create a record from memory—and vowed to
remember that I was there to work, not for the ride.

Yet it turned out to be a wild ride indeed. When I arrived
in Washington in January 1989 there was simply no way to
predict the historic events that I'd witness and help shape. At
the beginning of the decade, Ronald Reagan had come to office determined to challenge Soviet power and had done so
successfully. In 1985, Mikhail Gorbachev rose to power as
General Secretary of the Communist Party of the Soviet
Union. Facing rapid internal decay, Gorbachev began to
loosen the reins of communist authority at home and to pursue a more conciliatory course abroad. This approach rapidly
reshaped the foreign-policy landscape.

While President Reagan (prodded by then–Secretary of
State George Shultz) had decided that Mikhail Gorbachev
was indeed a different Soviet leader, some, including Brent
and myself, were skeptical of how authentic the shift in Soviet policy really was. To get a better feel for the changes that
were taking place in the Soviet Union and Eastern Europe,
we did a policy review of U.S.-Soviet relations and American relations with Eastern Europe.

While we were holding meetings, though, history was
sprinting ahead. In April, the Communist Party of Poland
was losing control of the country and called for negotiations

with Lech Walesa's underground Solidarity trade union. It seemed that the talks would end in a power-sharing arrangement that heavily advantaged the Solidarity workers and committed the Polish government to hold free parliamentary elections. There was an internal debate in Washington about how to respond. The State Department urged caution and recommended taking only tiny steps toward the emerging democratic forces. But the outcome of the negotiations would, I thought, be a turning point. Working quietly with several other staffers, I managed to get the President to take a more aggressive line.

Within a few days, President Bush went to Hamtramck, Michigan, to give a speech on Poland. The site was chosen by the domestic side of the White House to honor one of the nation's largest Polish American communities. I accompanied the President, riding for the first time on Air Force One. When I got home, I called Daddy and gave him a thorough account of the day, including the lunch on the second floor of a miserably hot Polish American restaurant. I didn't tell him that the President had mispronounced the phrase "Polish people," calling them instead the "polish people"—as in furniture wax. At that slip, Brent turned to me and barked, "Did you forget to capitalize the *P*?" I was mortified and took responsibility, though in fact the *P had* been capitalized. It was my first experience with the maxim that I would later pass on to NSC staffers: "It's the President's triumph and the NSC staffer's fault."

Over the next two months we finished our policy reviews, and the President delivered a couple of speeches loosely based on them. The effort to define a new course for

U.S.-Soviet relations laid out a series of benchmarks that the Soviets would have to meet in order to show that they were serious about change (although we had to keep revising the speeches because of how fast the situation was changing). From then on, even the most cautious among us knew that the changes were real. Now it was just a question of how far the Soviets were willing to go. Or more correctly, it was a question of whether Gorbachev was any longer in a position to stop the cascade of events that he had unleashed.

Even though I'd been stretched thin by events since arriving at the White House, I continued my long-standing practice of talking to my father on the phone every night, and I could tell that his life was increasingly intertwined with that of Clara Bailey, a principal in the Ravenswood school district where Daddy was volunteering. Ironically, Clara had been born in Birmingham too. An attractive, quiet, churchgoing Baptist lady, Clara was divorced with one grown son, Greg. I'd gotten to know her before leaving for Washington and noticed that Daddy seemed to favor her over the many ladies who sought his attention.

One night when I called him, Daddy's voice was halting. "I'd hoped to talk to you about this in person," he said, "but you're so busy, I don't know when you're coming home. Clara and I want to get married." He abruptly fell silent, waiting a second or so for me to respond. But before I could say anything he started talking again about how his love for my mother had been so special and nothing would ever replace that.

"Daddy, I know that," I said. I told him that I liked Clara

and was glad that they'd decided to get married. Frankly, it never occurred to me to question his decision.

The formal wedding was set for July 1, 1989, at Clara's house in Palo Alto. Greg and I were the witnesses, and I arranged to host the reception at the Stanford Faculty Club. At the reception, I realized that Daddy had made many new friends since my departure for Washington, and that was gratifying. Clara was clearly very good for him: compassionate and kind, she gave him a new lease on life. To this day she and I remain close. I must admit, though, that I felt a tinge of remorse at the wedding. I was glad that Daddy had found a companion, but his marriage opened the wound again of my mother's untimely death at the too-young age of sixty-one.

chapter thirty-six

I stayed in Palo Alto for just two days. With the quickening pace of international events, I simply couldn't afford any more time off. President Bush had decided to visit Eastern Europe in order to signal American support for what was unfolding there. Any doubts about the momentous nature of the changes were wiped away when we arrived in Poland on July 9 and in Hungary two days later.

Hungary had been a center of reform, managing even in the depths of the Cold War to gain some modicum of independence from Moscow. But now the Hungarians were challenging Soviet power directly and moving toward multiparty elections. More astonishingly, Hungary had decided to dismantle the barbed wire demarcating its border with Austria. In fact, during our time in Budapest, Hungarian Prime Minister Miklós Németh gave President Bush a piece of that twisted metal border fence. He proudly and rightly told the

President that his country had been the first to breach the Iron Curtain.

It was in Poland, though, that the Cold War had begun in 1945, and it was now clear that it was in Poland where it could end. Air Force One landed on a muggy, hot evening in Warsaw. Wojciech Jaruzelski, the communist general who'd imposed martial law in 1981 and was now the president of Poland, greeted President Bush. But communism in Poland had lost its ferocity. That night at the state dinner, held in a tacky, faded dining hall, the room suddenly went dark due to a power surge caused by the hot television lights. It was a metaphor for the Communist Party's coming fate.

It was clear that the party's demise was sealed the next day when we went to the city of Gdańsk, the home of Solidarity. In contrast to the stultifying arrival ceremony, President Bush was greeted in the town square by hundreds of thousands of cheering Polish workers. "Bush, Bush, Bush!" they chanted, waving American flags. "Freedom! Freedom! Freedom!"

I turned to a colleague and said, "I don't think this is what Karl Marx had in mind when he said, 'Workers of the world, unite.'"

By the end of August 1989, it was clear that the cascade of events would not stop in Poland and Hungary but would roll into Germany, the epicenter of the Cold War, and sweep away the line that had divided East from West for more than forty years, ever since the end of World War II.

At the time, the division of Germany into two parts was one of those givens of international politics. Each year West

German leaders would mechanically repeat platitudes about the coming day when all Germany would be united. But nobody actually believed it. Although the two countries had learned to live next to each other, their continued division hardly bred stability; the best troops of NATO and the best troops of the Warsaw Pact stood stationed on high alert at the border between East and West. Even with the collapse of communism in Poland and Hungary, few believed that the Soviet Union was ready to contemplate the unification of Germany.

By the fall of 1989, the impact of Gorbachev's policies was becoming evident. Erich Honecker, the hard-line leader of East Germany, had been forced from power because he was unwilling to pursue Moscow's liberalizing policies at home. Now, because of the refusal of other Warsaw Pact states, particularly Hungary, to enforce the border controls between their countries, hundreds fled East Germany without fear of being returned to the German Democratic Republic— the official name of a country that was anything but democratic. The flow quickened until it was a veritable flood. One news cartoon, captioned "Germany Unifies," depicted West Germany full of people and East Germany empty. That wasn't far from reality.

The GDR was dying, and increasingly Germans were speaking about what had only months before seemed impossible. I attended a conference in Germany at the end of October. Usually these transatlantic meetings were filled with talk of arms control and relations between the Warsaw Pact and NATO. This time, however, Germans wanted to talk to each other across the political divides of socialist and conservative, East and West. As an American, I felt like a bystander. On the plane ride home, I penned a memo for the President reporting that German unification was suddenly on the agenda. But before I could send it, the unthinkable happened: the Berlin Wall fell.

It turns out that the most momentous event in forty years of international history occurred thanks to a gigantic bureaucratic screw-up in the GDR. To stem the exodus of its citizens, the East German government decided to develop new, liberalized travel policies that would give East Germans the ability to leave the country. The hope was that in making it easier to travel back and forth, people would visit other nations but ultimately return home. Interior Ministry officials intended to have these relaxed restrictions apply to the border between East and West Germany, but *not* in Berlin, which had a different status. That point, however, was somehow left out of the draft regulations.

The new policies were written on November 9, 1989, but the internal security forces didn't yet have clear instructions on how to implement them. That night the party press secretary spotted the draft policies on a table as he headed to the podium for what had become a daily press conference to try to calm the waters. He read the regulations to the astonished press and almost immediately realized that he couldn't explain what they meant. But it was too late. People began to flock to the Berlin Wall, which for decades had been both the symbol and the reality of Europe's division. The Interior Ministry guards didn't know what to do. Faced with the flood of people, the commander made a historic decision: he ordered his troops to withhold fire. The Berlin Wall collapsed in joyous celebration.

At about three that afternoon Washington time, the phone rang in our suite of offices in the Old Executive Office Building, the place within the White House complex where most of the President's staff works. The assistant to Brent's deputy was on the phone. "The General"—as we called Brent—"wants you to come over and talk to the President about what is going on in Berlin," she said. Unfortunately, we had all been too busy doing other things to know what was happening. "Turn on CNN," she told us. "The Wall has come down."

My colleagues quickly made calls to the CIA and the State Department to verify what was being reported while I monitored the news coverage. Within a short time we were in Brent Scowcroft's office, trying to recover from the fact that the crack staff of the NSC had been scooped by CNN. The President was already in the Oval Office with the press. He was careful and guarded in his public reaction to the unfolding events, telling reporters that he was very pleased with the development. "We are saluting those who can move forward with democracy," the President said. "We are encouraging the concept of a Europe whole and free." These words were deliberately measured so as not to alarm the Soviets or get too far ahead of the West Germans in pushing for reunification. In private conversations within the West Wing, however, his support for unification was unequivocal. Nevertheless, when we suggested on that momentous day that President Bush go to Berlin, as Kennedy and Reagan had done, the President demurred. "This is a German moment," he said with characteristic modesty. "What would I do? Dance on the Wall?"

The next day, we began to consider how we would manage the unification process. We knew where we stood, thanks to the President's clarity. But the French and British weren't so sure that it was a good idea. Was Moscow really prepared to see Germany unify, and on what terms? We wanted to be sensitive to Soviet interests. After all, with about thirty-five thousand nuclear weapons and nearly five million men under arms, the Soviet Union was a weakening but still formidable force. The United States would need to be Germany's anchor and advocate. But we would also need to make sure that U.S. interests were protected. The Cold War was almost won after forty years. We didn't want to make a fatal mistake at the very end.

President Bush decided that he needed to sit down with Gorbachev. Perhaps naively, we hoped to arrange a low-key meeting between the two and worked with the Soviets to hold talks in the island country of Malta on December 2 and 3, 1989. The arrangements were to be kept secret until the last minute to prevent too much buildup. But we could not keep a meeting between the two world leaders quiet, and when the news leaked, the expectations for the summit were even greater, since the secrecy itself fueled speculation about what would happen.

At this meeting the President and Gorbachev started to develop a relationship of trust, which served them well through the coming metaphorical storms at the end of the

Cold War. It was also at this meeting that I met the Soviet leader for the first time.

"She tells me everything I need to know about the Soviet Union," the President said to Gorbachev as he introduced me.

"I certainly hope she knows a lot," Gorbachev quipped.

At the end of May 1990, Gorbachev came to Washington for a full-scale summit, his popularity in the West growing even as it declined at home. We wanted to make the visit special to shore up the Soviet president, whom we now saw as essential to ending the Cold War peacefully. There was a grand ceremony to sign an arms control treaty in the East Room, a magnificent state dinner, and a trip to Camp David, all underscoring the importance of the man and his excellent relationship with President Bush.

Gorbachev had been invited to give a speech at Stanford, and the President asked me to accompany Gorbachev to Palo Alto. As I sat on the South Lawn of the White House waiting with Gorbachev and his wife, Raisa, to take off in the presidential helicopter, Marine One, a thought crossed my mind: *I'm awfully glad I changed my major.*

chapter thirty-seven

By October 3, 1990, Germany unified fully within NATO. With Eastern Europe liberated, it was time to think about returning to Stanford. Most universities allow a faculty member to take only two consecutive years of leave without forfeiting tenure. Stanford had been very flexible in my case, and I felt that I needed to get back to my academic career. I was also dead tired.

I went to see Brent in September 1990 and told him that I needed to leave the NSC at the first of the year. He asked me to stay, saying that he wanted to restructure the staff in light of international events. Moreover, Saddam Hussein had invaded Kuwait that August, and the United States had rallied an international coalition against him. It was likely that there would be war in the Middle East. I told him that I'd stay a little while longer to help set up the new structure in light of the coming Gulf War, particularly since Moscow was confronting grave difficulty in managing the republics that were part of the Soviet Union. This was especially true of the Baltic states, which were suddenly restive, having seen the collapse of Soviet power in Europe. "Brent," I said, "the Soviet Union may break up, and I don't think I have the energy for it."

I did stay until April 1991. During the first part of that year, the Soviet Union's decline accelerated precipitously. We decided that the President needed to meet Soviet leaders other than Gorbachev, who was caught between the backlash of alarmed conservatives struggling to halt or even reverse the flow of events and the rise of radical figures who wanted to move faster even if it meant the end of the Soviet Union.

Boris Yeltsin was one of those radical leaders. He was making a claim—outlandish at the time—that Russia needed to be liberated from the Soviet Union. Yeltsin was Gorbachev's bitter rival, and when he requested a meeting with President Bush in September 1990, there was some reluctance to see him. The President had enormous respect and sympathy for Gorbachev and was determined to do nothing to embarrass the Soviet leader. We settled on a tried-and-true remedy for such a problem: a meeting with the national security advisor, during which the President would make an unannounced drop-by. Yeltsin was told only that he would meet Brent.

That afternoon I met Boris Yeltsin at the West Wing basement door. He got out of the car and turned to his aide. "This isn't the door you go in to see the President," he said in Russian. Obviously he'd expected to be received at the columned formal entrance to the White House where the Marine guards stand vigil.

Before the translator could say anything, I replied in Russian that Mr. Yeltsin's meeting was with General Scowcroft.

"Who is this man Scowcroft?" Yeltsin barked. "Is he even important enough to meet with me?" Yeltsin, a big man—more than six feet tall and at least 250 pounds—stood there with his arms folded, red-faced and scowling.

I was furious. "Mr. Yeltsin," I said, this time in English, "General Scowcroft is a busy man. If you don't want to keep your appointment, let me know and I'll cancel it and you can go back to your hotel."

He muttered to himself for a few moments, then huffed and said sharply, "Where is he?" I took him by the arm and almost dragged him up to Brent's office.

Brent, knowing none of this, greeted him warmly. Yeltsin sat down and launched into a soliloquy on his plans for Russia. Brent, who always worked too hard for his own good, fell asleep. Yeltsin didn't notice, completely absorbed in his own presentation. About thirty minutes into the meeting, the President flung open the door. Yeltsin smiled broadly, jumped up, and embraced the startled leader of the free world in a bear hug. Then he continued his monologue. After about thirty minutes more he was done. The President left, and I escorted a self-satisfied Yeltsin out to his car.

My first impressions of the man were obviously not very good. But less than a year later Yeltsin stood bravely atop a tank on a Moscow street and faced down the army and the security services of the Soviet Union. Boris Yeltsin would become the historic if somewhat flawed figure who brought down the Soviet Union and launched democracy in Russia. I was very glad that we had arranged that early meeting—bizarre as it was—with the President of the United States.

As expected, January 1991 brought the outbreak of war with Saddam Hussein. This event dominated the news and the attention of the President and Brent. But I was consumed with simultaneous crises in the Baltic states. Suddenly faced with the prospect of Baltic independence, Gorbachev belatedly tried to crack down. Thirteen people were killed and more than a hundred were wounded when Soviet-backed Lithuanian security forces fired on and drove tanks over protesters in Vilnius, the capital city. Violence in the Baltics continued to escalate. "We condemn these acts," President Bush told the press, saying that the events "could not help but affect our relationship" with Moscow. In spite of all the upheaval, however, the Soviet Union did not launch a full-scale military invasion of Lithuania and Latvia. I can't be sure, but I have always thought that the President's clarity helped to remind Moscow of the costs of doing so. After the events that January, it was increasingly clear that the Baltic states would become independent and that Gorbachev's days were numbered.

Fortunately, our pressure on Moscow did not disrupt the Gulf War coalition, which, led by American military power, successfully expelled Saddam Hussein's forces from Kuwait.

But the war left the Iraqi dictator in power, able to threaten his neighbors and oppress his people. That would be a problem for another day.

With the war concluded, I decided that I had discharged my duties and could return home. The President sent me a lovely letter recounting the role that I had played. "While the fate of the Soviet Union is still not decided," he wrote, "you have set us on a course to realize the historic dream of a Europe whole, free and at peace." I was sad to leave but felt a tremendous sense of completion and accomplishment.

The day before my departure, First Lady Barbara Bush invited me to join her for tea in the residence. "You are such a good friend of the Bushes," she said. "This won't be the last that we see of you."

chapter thirty-eight

I returned to Stanford tired but content. The university was again generous, telling me that I would not be required to teach until the fall quarter. That allowed me time to design my next research project—the one that I would use to make my case for promotion to full professor during the next academic year.

I didn't miss Washington or the work in the White House. Even when the coup against Gorbachev took place in August 1991, leading to the eventual collapse of the Soviet Union in December, I didn't regret my decision to leave. Throughout the spring and summer I worked again for ABC News as an expert analyst but largely kept my distance from the policy world.

One of my surprises upon returning to Palo Alto was just how much my father had established a new life and reputation of his own. Daddy had always been a magnet for people, and he'd become a powerful one in Palo Alto. Not only was he active with Stanford's Public Service Center and the Department of Athletics, transforming what was once just a study hall for freshman football players into an academic resource and tutoring center for all Stanford athletes, but he had also become a well-regarded figure in East Palo Alto.

Not long after I returned home, one of Daddy's new friends—Charlie Mae Knight, the superintendent of the Ravenswood schools in East Palo Alto—asked if I would deliver the districtwide commencement address. Ravenswood is an elementary and middle school district with no high school. Yet as I was sitting on the stage, it occurred to me that with extended families having come from all over the Bay Area and beyond to attend the ceremonies, the commencement exercises felt more like a high school graduation.

"This is an awfully elaborate commencement for eighth graders," I said to Charlie.

"Well," she said, "that's because seventy percent of these kids will never finish high school. This is their last commencement."

I was stunned, and realized that I knew very little of the poverty and lack of opportunity just a few blocks from my house.

That evening, I asked my father to tell me about the challenges for the school district, feeling a little embarrassed that I'd lived in the area for ten years and knew nothing, while my father, who'd moved to Palo Alto only recently, was actively trying to help. He told me about some of his efforts, including refurbishing an athletic field for the district. Daddy also told me about what Charlie Mae wanted to do. Ravenswood had had eleven superintendents in ten years and the odds were long, but he was impressed with her toughness and commitment. He was going to be a partner to her and mobilize resources from Stanford to help. "Stanford has been running its own programs and its own agenda in East Palo Alto," he said. "It's about time that someone ask the people there what they need."

My father was just doing what he'd done all of his life: following in his father's footsteps of educational evangelism. I resolved right then to get involved too, and asked Charlie Mae to lunch a few days later. She talked about the need for extended-day learning activities, saying that children had nothing wholesome to do after school. Most extracurricular activities such as music and art had been cut because of budgetary pressures. Charlie and I agreed that I'd pull together some people who might be interested in helping, and after some discussions a group of community leaders from Palo Alto planned to launch the Center for a New Generation (CNG).

We had no idea how hard it would be. There was a political power structure in East Palo Alto that was suspicious of outsiders and determined to keep control. It didn't help that I was from Stanford, which, as my father had noted, had a well-deserved reputation for giving the help they decided the community needed without asking the community what it wanted. There were also a number of nonprofits in East Palo Alto run by residents of the city that were little more than jobs programs for the staffs of the organizations. Money had flowed to these programs from corporations and foundations with little demand for accountability. In this way, Palo

Alto had eased its conscience, but it was hard to argue that kids were being helped by what my dad called "guilt money." Some of the directors of these programs, who were often powerful people in the city, saw the CNG as a threat to their funding sources.

To break through, we had to work very hard. We held community meetings, and also scheduled numerous meetings with the Board of Education. We brought the chair of the school board into the effort, which helped immensely. And we addressed the city council. I finally lost my cool when one of the members asked what was in it for me. I shot back, "Nothing. But there *is* something in it for your kids. Why are you so hard to help?"

The experience taught me many tough lessons about the difficulties of community organizing and the power of entrenched interests. I also learned that nonprofit management could be an oxymoron; several of the staff members possessed good hearts but little management skill. But by the summer of 1992 we were able to launch the program for children in grades five to eight. Each summer 250 kids were exposed to hands-on math and science instruction, language arts, instrumental music, dance, and art. The curriculum was repeated as an after-school program for 150 kids. We hired the best teachers from the school district and paid them very well, hoping they'd take the innovative curriculum back into their regular classrooms. College students, including many athletes from Stanford, acted as mentors for the kids. The students were chosen on the basis of teacher recommendation, but we were determined that the program be not just for the "talented tenth" or for remedial education. Instead, it was conceived of as an enrichment program.

The crown jewels of the program were the instrumental bands, which made me remember how important bands were to my black heritage in the segregated South. Today there are five Centers for a New Generation spread across East Palo Alto, East Menlo Park, and now heavily Hispanic Redwood City, and they have partnered with the Boys and Girls Clubs of America. I particularly enjoyed working with Daddy to bring these programs into being, and I am sure my grandfather John Wesley Rice Sr. noted and approved of the way the experience sparked my own determination to be an educational evangelist.

Though I was very busy, I also made four trips to Russia during this period, enjoying my freedom to visit the country as a faculty member rather than a government official. These were important visits as I saw firsthand the disorientation and humiliation of the Russian population after the collapse of the Soviet Union. Years later, that extended time in Russia helped me to understand the appeal of Vladimir Putin, who promised Russians order, prosperity and respect.

Like most at Stanford, I was following with some interest the impending change in leadership at the university. The school had gotten into a dispute with the federal government about payments for costs associated with government contracts. It was a headline-grabbing scandal, with charges that Stanford had overbilled the government to the tune of $200 million. Don Kennedy, who for ten years had been the highly successful leader of the university and to whom I had been quite close, decided to step down.

I didn't expect to be appointed to the committee that would choose the next president. After all, I'd been away from Stanford three out of the last four years. But one day in September I received a call from the chairman of the Board of Trustees. "We need you to help find a new president," he said. "This is going to be a tough process because the university is really hurting and a lot of people don't like the direction it has been going in. And I hate to tell you this, but it will take a lot of time. Will you serve?" I readily accepted.

Before joining the search committee I hadn't known how many difficulties Stanford was facing. There had been massive budgetary cuts and layoffs as the federal government slashed payments to the university amid the dispute. Moreover, there was a serious rift between conservative alumni and the school. Conservative faculty were also disaffected, feeling that the university was compromising academic excellence in the service of political correctness.

One of the precipitating events occurred in 1988, when the university had ended the core humanities curriculum, called Western Civilization. Western Civ had been deemed to be about "dead white men" and therefore unacceptable for a multiethnic, multiracial, multigendered campus. The course had been replaced with Culture, Ideas and Values, also known as CIV, without the offending "Western" preceding it. CIV's curriculum required race, class, and gender components and at least one book by a "woman of color."

The rifts became chasms when Stanford rejected the request of the family of Ronald Reagan to establish his presidential library on campus. Ostensibly, the excuse was traffic congestion at the site, but everyone knew that it had been the agitation of a small but vocal faculty group that forced the university to turn down the library.

Stanford wasn't exactly falling apart, but it was a very polarized place. There was even a split concerning intercollegiate athletics, with some saying that the university's commitment to Division I sports meant a lowering of academic standards. The new president obviously would have a lot of work to do.

After several months, the search committee identified a handful of prospects with the unquestioned academic credentials and administrative experience that would be required of Stanford's president. Then we took to the road to interview the candidates. No sitting university president or provost wants to be identified as a candidate for a job, only to fail to be selected. Thus we always disguised our travel to avoid leaks about who was being considered.

A group of us were sent to Chicago to interview Gerhard Casper, the provost of the University of Chicago. After about an hour during which Gerhard, an eminent constitutional lawyer, quizzed us as much as we did him, he turned to me. "You are representative of the next generation of leadership at Stanford," he said. "What do you think is the greatest challenge?" I answered that the university had strayed from its core purposes and was trying to do too much.

The discussions continued, and as we walked out of Gerhard's apartment and into the frigid Chicago night, I turned to a fellow committee member and said, "I could work for him."

The committee deliberated for a few more weeks, but well ahead of schedule we decided that Gerhard Casper was likely the right man to lead Stanford. He came to Los Angeles to meet the committee one last time in secret. There we had a truly open and frank discussion. Gerhard was known as a conservative with very traditional views of the role of the university. The University of Chicago didn't even have intercollegiate athletics. We worried that there might be some issues with the fit between this distinguished silver-haired German immigrant and northern California's informality. I even asked Gerhard if he believed in affirmative action, citing my own case as one that had worked out pretty well. He said that he did, explaining that he believed diversity and excellence were not enemies. After several hours, we were comfortable with our choice. We believed that Gerhard saw Stanford's unique strengths and that he'd put the university back on course. And he wouldn't try to make our beloved university into something it didn't want to be.

chapter thirty-nine

Gerhard took the reins in September of 1992. I was friendly with Gerhard and his wife, Regina, and Gerhard would consult me from time to time about various university matters. I also took it upon myself to make sure Gerhard became intimately acquainted with Stanford sports. When Stanford played the number-one-ranked University of Washington, Gerhard asked me to join him in the president's box. The game was at night and, with television time-outs, was going on quite long. But Bill Walsh's Stanford team was somehow still in the game late in the fourth quarter against the heavily favored Huskies.

As Stanford took the ball for one last drive, Gerhard turned to me and said, "It's late. I'm going to go home now."

I couldn't believe it. "Gerhard," I said, taking him by the arm, "if you leave now, your presidency is over." He was a little startled but stayed as Stanford went on to a remarkable win.

Because of our relationship, I didn't think much of it when my secretary came in to say that Gerhard wanted me to come to lunch one day; I knew the university was looking for a new provost, and I figured they'd settled on a candidate and he wanted to get my opinion.

When I arrived, Gerhard and I went into his sunny office and sat across from each other at the round table. After a few pleasantries he said, "I want you to become the provost of the university."

I literally dropped my forkful of tuna back into the bowl. "This is a joke, right?"

His eyes twinkled a bit and he smiled. "No, Condi. I want you to become the provost."

Perhaps to give me a moment to recover, he launched into a discussion of why he thought I should be provost. "I've decided that it's time to skip a generation in leadership here at Stanford," he said, referring obliquely to the numerous deans and department chairs undoubtedly expecting to be named provost. "After your experience in Washington, and having gotten to know you, I think you're the right person to help me lead Stanford. In fact, I knew it the moment we met in Chicago."

Gerhard then addressed my unspoken concern by saying that he was not making the appointment because I was a black woman, although he was delighted that I'd be the first to hold the job. He added that, at thirty-eight, I was also going to be the youngest provost by almost a decade. From his point of view, that would be the real issue, not my race or gender. He could have added that I had never been a department chair, let alone a dean—or he could have mentioned that I'd been promoted to full professor only about a month before.

The provost of Stanford has broad-ranging responsibilities for the academic program, the physical plant, and the budget. The deans report to the provost, along with most other senior officials of the university. Provosts' responsibilities vary from university to university, but the Stanford job is probably the most powerful and broadest in all of academia. And these were not ordinary times. Stanford faced crippling challenges, and the provost would be expected to solve them.

I told Gerhard that I'd think about it overnight and call him the next day. As I made my way back to my office, memories flooded back of walking along the same colonnade as an insecure graduate student going to my first interview so many years before. I knew that I'd say yes and become provost—even though I was still totally stunned to have been asked.

I imagined how the news would be received on campus. Not only was I young, black, and female, but I was a Republican on a campus where that is rare. I focused on what messages I wanted to send to the faculty, the students, the alumni, and the trustees. The next day I went to see Gerhard and accepted the job.

The news was received somewhat better than I expected. People were surprised, of course, but with the exception of some grousing by a few faculty members about my being a conservative, there wasn't much negative reaction. I no longer felt much trepidation about what was to come. In fact,

I was pretty excited. A couple of days later I found myself driving through campus singing along with the theme from the early-eighties TV series *The Greatest American Hero*: "Believe it or not, I'm walking on air / I never thought I could feel so free / Flying away on a wing and a prayer / Who could it be? / Believe it or not, it's just me."

My most important responsibility as provost would be dealing with the university's financial situation. I had to cut $20 million from the budget immediately. Moreover, the university needed money to rebuild the campus after the Loma Prieta earthquake in 1989 had left the university severely damaged. All the easy budget cuts had already been made, I told the Faculty Senate, so we'd have to make significant cuts. "I don't do committees," I said. "I'll consult widely. But someone will have to make decisions, and that will be Gerhard and me."

There was a bit of a rumble through the room, but I don't think anyone really believed me. It didn't matter. I had made a promise to the trustees that I would balance the budget, and I was determined to do it.

Predictably, the pushback came from groups that had felt privileged and untouchable for political reasons. The ethnic centers (Asian American, African American, Chicano, and Native American) were the most offended. The protests heated up, and they called a town-hall-style meeting and asked me to attend. I expected a huge, angry crowd, and that's what I got.

After a few strong words about how marginalized and victimized the ethnic students were feeling, the president of Stanford's Black Student Union handed me the microphone.

I resisted the temptation to say that I thought *marginalization* was a peculiar term for students who'd been given the chance at a Stanford education. Instead, I plunged into a presentation of the financial situation, saying that I'd asked the Physics Department for the same budget analysis. Everyone had to contribute.

During the question-and-answer session, a young woman yelled, "The problem is, you just don't care enough for the plight of minorities." The audience erupted in cheers. Then, not really having thought it through, I said, "You don't have the standing to question my commitment to minorities. I've been black all of my life, and that is far longer than you are old." The buzzing told me that I'd hit a nerve. The young woman sat down. I said a few words more and prepared to leave. But as I was turning away, the moderator decided that he would have the last word. I went back and took the microphone from him. "When you are the provost, you can have the last word," I said. Then I left, feeling that I'd established necessary boundaries.

Throughout this difficult period, the headlines about me were brutal and the criticism came almost daily. I talked to Daddy every day, and he brought the perspective of someone who'd been through tough decisions in a university environment. I know that the barrage of criticism directed at me, some of it quite personal, bothered him. I assured Daddy that I wasn't worried about the headlines, but he was concerned nonetheless. His reaction at that time has caused me to wonder how he would have dealt with my encounters with the rough-and-tumble environment of Washington when I was national security advisor and then secretary of state. I am sure he would have gotten through it, but I could tell that Daddy hated to see his "little girl" demonized.

Nonetheless, Daddy also helped me to see the student protests in a different light. He believed it important for students to find their political voices while in the university. He reminded me that they were, after all, quite young. I realized that Daddy was right when, shortly before graduation, the student who had moderated the town hall came to see me and asked how he could be more effective at leadership. In the classroom, I was always careful not to put a student down for a comment, no matter how inappropriate. To do so is to freeze the rest of the students, who will fear humiliation. The power relationship is unequal, and students feel it. I decided that I'd try to remember that in my encounters with them as provost. In any case, I had established a pretty tough line. Maybe it was time to back off.

The budget situation took most of my time, but I had to attend to other matters as well. A few games into the football season, Bill Walsh, the legendary coach who had returned to Stanford after extraordinary successes in the NFL, asked to see me for dinner on the Sunday after a home game. He had found the return to Stanford hard and ultimately unsatisfying. Initially, his team had been very successful, defeating Notre Dame at South Bend in the first year. But now, in his third year, Stanford's football fortunes had taken a turn for the worse. The talent was thin and the execution flawed. Bill was in no mood to do what it would take to revive the program: spend days and weeks on the road trying to recruit players to come to Stanford. He was tired.

I told Walsh that I didn't need one of sports' greatest legends quitting five games into the season. I implored him to stay on, saying we'd do a proper search as soon as the season was over. In the end he stayed until the end of the season. We then launched a search for Bill's successor. Tyrone Willingham, who'd been an assistant at Stanford and was now with the Minnesota Vikings, emerged as a top candidate. "We are going to be criticized for his inexperience," I told Gerhard. "But everyone says he was great when he was here, and we all believe he'll be a fabulous recruiter."

"Do it," Gerhard said. Then he added with a chuckle, "I don't worry too much about being criticized for appointing inexperienced people."

The press conference announcing Ty's appointment was set for the next day. I woke up that morning and went down to get the paper. In the sports section I saw that Glenn Dickey of the *San Francisco Chronicle* had written that Stanford was about to hire an inexperienced coach because I'd insisted on bringing on a black person. I was furious and called Glenn. "You didn't say that the University of Colorado hired Rick Neuheisel [who had also not been a coordinator] because he was blond," I told him.

I also called Ty, who said that it wasn't the first time he'd been underestimated. Willingham would go on to be one of Stanford's most successful coaches, returning the Cardinal to the Rose Bowl in 2000 for the first time in twenty-eight years. Glenn Dickey later apologized, admitting that he'd been wrong about Willingham.

The truth is, issues of affirmative action are tricky in a university, whether in admissions, in faculty hiring and tenure, or in selecting a football coach. There is probably no single issue on which I've felt more misunderstood. For instance, I have been called an opponent of affirmative action. In fact, I'm a supporter of affirmative action—if done in what I consider to be the right way. No one can doubt that years of racial prejudice produced underrepresentation of minorities and women in all aspects of American life. Corporate boardrooms, management suites, and elite university faculties and student bodies have for our entire history failed to reflect even roughly the ethnic mix of the country. That is not acceptable in America, which is the world's greatest multiethnic democracy.

Yet the question of how to remedy that situation is a delicate one. I've always believed that there are plenty of qualified minorities for these roles—even some who are "twice as good." But the processes of selection, the networks through which people are identified, can very easily be insular and produce the same outcomes over and over. The answer lies in looking outside established networks and patterns of hiring. I consistently told the Stanford community quite openly that affirmative action had figured in my own case. Stanford traditionally found its faculty at peer institutions such as Harvard or Yale or perhaps the University of California—not at the University of Denver. But when, through the Ford Fellowship, I appeared on the radar screen, Stanford took a chance on me as an assistant professor. I always closed by saying that it had worked out just fine for me and for the university.

Unfortunately, very few minorities—particularly blacks, Latinos, and Native Americans—go to graduate school, the pool from which assistant professors are selected. I had to make this somewhat unpopular point frequently to defend the relatively meager number of minorities we hired onto the faculty in any given year, though those numbers increased during my tenure. When pressed by minority students, I'd ask for a show of hands regarding how many were going on to graduate school. Few hands would go up. I'd then tell them that I couldn't create assistant professors out of whole cloth and that they should consider going to graduate school. And we tried vigorously to recruit good minority students to our graduate programs. Very often, though, we found ourselves competing for the same few black or Latino students who'd been identified by our peers, Harvard, Yale, and so on.

It is also true that in student admissions it is necessary to take race into account. I don't know why, but minorities continue to score lower on standardized tests. Even after we adjust for socioeconomic status, this disparity holds. But as my own story about the results of my PSAT in high school shows, these tests are not fully predictive of a student's success or failure. Over the years I have had students with perfect records at entry fail and students who were thought to have been marginal succeed. Yet the idea that minority students are getting a break at the expense of white students is one of the most toxic issues of our time.

The key to affirmative action, I believe, is not to lower standards but to look for good prospects where you would not ordinarily find them. Yet there are pitfalls with the whole concept of affirmative action. There is the stigma that is easily attached to minorities simply because there is a widespread belief that affirmative action figured heavily in every case. This leads to what President George W. Bush called (in the context of elementary and secondary education) the "soft bigotry of low expectations." Many times, well-meaning faculty would say that they were taking extra time with their "remedial students" to help them catch up. A little investigation would typically reveal that these professors equated "remedial" with "minority." When I attended my first Phi Beta Kappa ceremony in 1994, I was surprised to see only two black inductees. I suspected that minority students were internalizing the message of inferiority and living down to the expectations that were being set for them.

I decided to start a program for freshman called Partners in Academic Excellence. Minority faculty and graduate students agreed to take fifteen or so minority freshmen to dinner once a week. The graduate students also mentored the freshman—for instance, by reading their class papers. My suspicions were confirmed when the black graduate students reported that the freshman were being given "courtesy" grades, higher than warranted so as not to affect their self-esteem. The problem, of course, was that easier grading early on left the students unprepared for the tougher subject matter that was coming.

Gerhard supported the program but worried that I was setting up a miniature "segregated" academic system within Stanford. Ironically, that was *exactly* what I was doing— trying to reproduce elements of my segregated childhood, when teachers did not worry about being called racists for their high expectations and "no victims" approach.

In time, we reworked the program to broaden its participation. We learned that student athletes suffered from the same prejudices, as did women students in math and the sciences. I was reminded again how difficult it is to overcome preconceptions and stereotypes—particularly for people who want so desperately to do the right thing for "those poor minorities and women."

I loved the regular rhythm of the provost's job, which gave me time to spend with Daddy. We continued to work together on the Center for a New Generation and saw it grow and prosper. I visited him at least twice a week, always going over after church on Sunday to watch sports, as we'd done so many years before. He and Clara and I went to Stanford football and basketball games together. Daddy loved my friends and became close to several of them. One day, standing on the practice field while watching spring football together, he turned to me and said, "I'm so glad I came here. Palo Alto is such a nice village. And it is awfully nice to be the father of one of the most important people in the village."

I realized at that moment that Daddy was finally enjoying the comforts of the retirement he deserved. His life had turned around since those dark days in Denver when his professional life crashed around him. It had been hard work rebuilding his life after Mother's death. But he had succeeded beyond my wildest dreams. In 1994, for his work on behalf of minority communities in Denver and East Palo Alto, the National Alliance of Black School Educators presented him with their Living Legend award. In 1998, the City of Palo Alto honored him with a lifetime achievement award. And the community college system in California still awards John W. Rice Jr. diversity fellowships every year.

* * *

As good as life was, I knew that my time as provost had to come to an end. Gerhard had been president for seven years and was starting to think about his successor. I loved being provost but didn't want to be president, even of Stanford, with the job's emphasis on conducting the external affairs of the university—alumni and government relations and fund-raising. Gerhard needed a new provost who could be groomed to succeed him.

I was also beginning to feel that I'd done all that I could do. My tenure had been somewhat controversial, but I don't doubt that the trustees appreciated the six budget surpluses I'd produced, the renewal of undergraduate education that Gerhard and I had championed, and the repair of the physical campus. Even the students had come to like me. When I announced I was stepping down from the post, the *Stanford Daily* ran an editorial entitled "Farewell, Provost Rice," which featured a line that I will always treasure: "Condi leaves a legacy as a powerful administrator who cares about students." Even the minority communities—particularly the black community—showed its appreciation with a wonderful farewell event, complete with gospel versions of my favorite hymns.

As for the faculty, I'm not so sure. I'd made a lot of tough decisions with directness and without showing much patience for the veto groups that populate a university faculty. Many colleagues called to say that they'd miss my clear and unapologetic leadership. Nonetheless, I'm sure that many others were relieved when, in the announcement of my decision to step down, I made clear that I was done with university administration. The fact that I'd signed on to help Governor George W. Bush in his run for the Presidency of the United States convinced everyone that I meant what I'd said. But I was absolutely truthful when, at the event held to honor my service, I said that being provost of Stanford was the best job I'd ever had.

chapter forty

The evening after Stanford's event in my honor, my father and I had dinner. He was a little pensive but jokingly said that maybe I'd have more time for dinner now that I was no longer going to be provost. Hearing that, I made a silent vow to see him more.

"So, what are you going to do for an encore?" he asked.

I explained that I liked management and the private sector and thought that I might try to combine the two.

"Aren't you going to help George W. Bush on foreign policy?" Daddy asked.

"Yes," I replied. "But that won't be full-time."

"Sure," Daddy said incredulously—and presciently.

My association with Governor Bush had begun in earnest in August 1998 when George H. W. Bush called to invite me to spend a little time with his son Governor George W. Bush, just so we could get to know each other better and talk a little about foreign policy.

When the then–Texas governor told me that he'd likely make a run for the White House, his presidential bid struck me as having long odds for success. The Clinton years had been morally tarnished but peaceful and relatively prosperous. The governor was untested and would likely face a real pro in Vice President Al Gore. I was too polite to say these things, but I sure thought them.

George W. Bush was still a few months from being reelected as Texas governor in a landslide victory, carrying 68 percent of the vote. He told me that he was confident of reelection and that if he won impressively (which he fully expected), he'd likely run for the Presidency. He wanted to start thinking about what to do in foreign policy if he got elected. Throughout the weekend, while fishing (he fished, I sat in the boat and watched) or exercising side by side in the small family gym on the compound, we talked about Russia, China, and Latin America. I soon realized that he knew our southern neighbors, particularly Mexico, far better than I did.

But we also talked about other things. He was interested in my upbringing in segregated Birmingham. I was attracted to his passion for improving education for disadvantaged youth.

We emailed back and forth several times during the fall, and a couple of days after the election, I received a note from him. From that time on, we began to follow international events together. In March 1999 I received a call asking if I'd come down to Austin to talk to the governor about the upcoming campaign. When my picture appeared on the front page of the *New York Times* as a member of the exploratory committee dedicated to electing George W. Bush President of the United States, my father was the first person I called.

The campaign itself proved professionally fulfilling, but early on I realized that it would require my full-time focus. Foreign policy would be the governor's Achilles' heel against more seasoned candidates in the primaries and, eventually, in the general election. I knew that George Bush would look to me to help answer the inevitable questions about his readiness to assume the mantle of commander in chief.

I was having fun. Anyone who's interested in politics should do a campaign from the ground floor at least once. I loved the pace and the sense of being a part of an adventure.

Then, in February 2000, Daddy suffered cardiac arrest. I was in a meeting when my assistant burst in and said that something had happened to Daddy. I rushed out and sped to his house. It looked like a scene from a TV medical drama. Daddy was on the floor and they were shocking his heart. I heard the medic say, "I have a weak pulse." We all rushed to the hospital and waited. It hadn't been a heart attack, but his heart had stopped long enough to deprive his brain of oxygen, and he was now in a coma. No one could say what the prognosis was.

Daddy continued in a coma for about a week and then he began to stir. But he'd sustained significant brain damage. A few times we were asked those awful questions about whether to continue life-sustaining support. Here I have to say that I was weaker than my stepmother, who was prepared to go to extraordinary lengths to keep my father alive. I just wasn't so sure and prayed every day and night for guidance about what to do.

Then one day I was in his room and the basketball game was on television. I thought I could see him tracking the game with his eyes. Not long after, Daddy began to improve, and eventually he was transferred to a nursing home for long-term care.

Soon after, I resumed my campaign activities. I called several times a day to check on Daddy, and friends took daily shifts to sit with my father. The nursing home had wonderful, caring attendants, but such facilities are woefully understaffed, so I never trusted the quality of care enough to leave him alone, even for a minute.

Sometimes Clara or my aunt Gee, my mother's sister who'd come out to help us, would put Daddy on the phone. He seemed to know that he was talking to me. I tried never to be away from home for too long, returning to help oversee his multiple therapies and feeding tubes or struggle with Medicare and insurance. And I would endure those terrible episodes when he would yell out for what seemed like hours. This was, according to the doctors, a good sign that his brain was repairing itself. To me it sounded as if my father was being flung into the depths of hell.

By the summer, Daddy's condition had improved somewhat more and we moved him home, with the help of wonderful caretakers. Daddy seemed to understand what was being said to him, but his responses were often off track. Yet at least he was home, where we could sing together and share the occasional flashes of lucidity that would come. Sometimes he'd amaze us all. On Thanksgiving as we gathered around his bed, my uncle Alto said, "Who is going to give the blessing?" Without missing a beat, Daddy reached somewhere deep into the recesses of his memory and prayed.

He never fully recovered, but he fought to live. Several times he was near death and refused to go. As I watched this giant of a man who'd loved me more than anything in the world approach the end, it was hard to find much good in life. It seemed so unfair that I could no longer share stories of the campaign with my father. Here I was at the height of my professional career, and my father couldn't enjoy it with me. Not surprisingly, my absences from home became a source of guilt for me, and the campaign, which had been such a thrill, became something of a slog. But I kept going and told myself that Daddy undoubtedly approved of my decision to keep my commitment to the campaign.

I flew down to Austin the afternoon of the election. By the time I arrived at the Four Seasons Hotel, the news stations were chalking up state after state in the Gore column. By the time I made it downstairs to watch with a few Bush friends and family, everything was going against us: Michigan, Illinois, Pennsylvania, and Florida were all gone. I sat there with Doro Bush Koch, the governor's sister, and watched in dismay. "Let's change places," I said to Doro, employing a superstition from my days as a sports fan. If your team is not winning while you're sitting on the right side of the sofa, move to the left. Yes, I know it doesn't matter, but it can't hurt.

We did change places. Then, almost magically, NBC

CONDOLEEZZA RICE

News reported that we had won Georgia. Next came reports that the news stations were going to reverse their call on Florida. Hours later the TV screen suddenly showed "George W. Bush, 43rd President of the United States." It was quite a moment. I wanted to call my father but decided not to, fearing that he would be too disoriented to share the moment with me.

I jumped into a minivan with other Bush supporters for the trip to the capitol for the victory speech. It was freezing cold in Austin, and we stood on the square, rocking to music and hugging each other. But something was wrong. Al Gore hadn't conceded. I could also see the big screen displaying CNN's election coverage. The margin of victory in Florida was shrinking very fast, and there would likely be a recount.

"You know what this is like?" I said to a friend. "It's like eating a really spicy meal before bed and having a bad dream. You think to yourself, 'Must have been what I ate last night. Boy, I'm glad to wake up from that one!'" But of course it wasn't a dream.

Governor Bush called the morning after the election to say that he wanted me to be national security advisor but that we'd obviously have to wait a bit on any announcement. It was surreal, but we went through the motions of planning a foreign policy transition that might never happen. One particularly bad idea was to have a photo op of the governor and me sitting in front of a fireplace discussing foreign policy. It looked like a faux Oval Office shot and was properly ridiculed. I decided to go home to California.

The return to California gave me a chance to spend quality time with my father. I watched the ups and downs in

288

Florida, my mood swinging with every court decision. Sometimes Daddy seemed to be tracking, becoming agitated and shedding tears when the news was bad.

I left on December 8 to attend a meeting of the foreign policy team in Washington. We were planning for the transition in case there was one. After the session, fellow campaign worker Steve Hadley and I were sitting in the conference room of his law office when we got word that the Florida Supreme Court had ordered a manual recount. As we headed over to a restaurant for dinner, I said, "Steve, I would have loved to serve with you. You would have been a great deputy national security advisor."

I flew home to California the next day believing that it was over. When I got off the plane and into the car, my driver gave me an update. The Supreme Court had by a 5–4 decision issued a stay, halting the manual recounts and setting a hearing for the matter on Monday, December 11. This meant that the judges in the majority were likely to rule in favor of Bush on the merits of the case, certifying Bush as the winner of Florida's electoral votes. George W. Bush would indeed become the 43rd President of the United States.

Three days before Christmas I stopped in to see Daddy on my way to dinner, and he seemed in pretty good spirits. I called a few hours later, and Daddy got on the phone. "I'm going home," he said.

"Daddy, you *are* at home," I answered.

"No, it's time for me to go home."

I knew in my heart what he meant, and it terrified me. My father, a Presbyterian minister and a man of great faith, believed that at the end of our earthly existence, God calls us home to eternal life.

I rushed to his house. He seemed fine, and I left to drive the ten minutes to my house. As I walked in the door, Clara was calling. Daddy had stopped breathing. We rushed to the hospital. This time the physical and mental damage were irreparable. On Christmas Eve, after slipping into a coma, my father died.

I'd told Daddy just after the election that George Bush wanted me to go to Washington and become national security advisor. He cried at the news, but I couldn't tell whether they were tears of joy for my achievement or tears of despair because he knew that we would be separated. With his death he resolved my dilemma. Was it coincidence? I've always prayed that it was, because I can't bear to think that John Wesley Rice Jr. deliberately did this one last thing to make sure I fulfilled my dreams. Honestly, it would have been just like him.

chapter forty-one

The funeral for my father stood in stark contrast to the private service for my mother. John Rice loved people and people loved him. Jerusalem Baptist Church, where Clara worshiped, was filled to the rafters. The pastor, Jonathan Staples, gave the eulogy. He was yet another young man whom my father had befriended and mentored. Clara and I sang "In the Garden," a song that my father had remembered and sung until the very end.

I come to the garden alone,
While the dew is still on the roses;
And the voice I hear, falling on my ear,
The Son of God discloses.

And He walks with me,
And He talks with me,

And He tells me that I am His own;
And the joy we share as we tarry there,
None other has ever known.

The service ended with a little jazz ensemble playing "When the Saints Go Marching In" for this son of Louisiana.

We laid Daddy to rest at Alta Mesa Memorial Gardens, not far from the Stanford campus, on December 28. A few years before, I'd moved my mother's remains from Denver to the same cemetery. When I decided to do so, my father had been very pleased. But he'd reminded me that the grave is not really a Christian's final resting place. "The Lord's eternal home is the final destination," he'd say. At the end of Daddy's life, I was comforted by my faith in the truth of what he had said and my belief that he and my mother were united again.

I left for Washington about a week later. There was so much to do as the new national security advisor. I told myself that I couldn't afford to be debilitated by my grief. I just powered through the meetings, the briefings, the calls, each day, determined to do what needed to be done. Yet since my mother's first bout with cancer I had wondered how it would feel to live without my parents. We had been so close. Would I ever feel whole again?

Oh, how I missed them. At the inauguration in 2001, I ached to have my parents sitting on the Mall watching George W. Bush take the oath of office, ushering me into the White House as well. When I landed in Moscow aboard a plane that simply said "The United States of America," I wanted to send them the photograph. Visiting the Holy Land, I thought of how much my father would have relished walking in the footsteps of Jesus Christ. Sitting in the Presidential Box at the Kennedy Center, I thought that my mother would have loved to see *Aïda* there and that my father would have hated it but gone along "for Ann's sake." And, of course, in 2010 I wanted my father to know that the New Orleans Saints had won the Super Bowl. He would have *loved* that!

But often it has been their presence, not their absence, that I've experienced. I could almost see John and Angelena Rice at the door of my West Wing office, as national security advisor, and hovering over me as I flew into a combat zone in Baghdad or Kabul as secretary of state. "You are well prepared for whatever is ahead of you," I could hear them say. "Now don't forget that you are God's child and He will keep you in His care." They remain by my side. And I feel today, as before, the overwhelming and unconditional love of the extraordinary, ordinary parents that I was so blessed to have.

chronology of events

1863 January 1: President Abraham Lincoln signs the Emancipation Proclamation, freeing slaves in Confederate states but leaving slavery intact in the North. It nevertheless makes the abolition of slavery a central objective of the Union forces in the Civil War.

1865–1877 The end of the Civil War marks the beginning of the Reconstruction era, a period during which the government tries to solve social, economic, and political problems brought about by the reunification of the Northern and Southern states.

1865 The United States ratifies the Thirteenth Amendment to the Constitution, which bans slavery and involuntary servitude.

1866 The Ku Klux Klan is formed in Tennessee by Confederate veterans of the Civil War.

1868 The Fourteenth Amendment to the Constitution grants civil and legal rights to all citizens of the United States and prevents those rights from being abridged or denied by any state.

1870 Hiram Revels of Mississippi is elected the first black U.S. senator.

1870 The Fifteenth Amendment to the Constitution gives African American men the right to vote by banning restrictions based on race or "previous condition of servitude"; women still cannot vote.

1870 Many Southern states begin passing so-called Jim Crow laws—laws that segregate public facilities, forbid marriage between races, and make voting almost impossible for people of color. Jim Crow was a stereotypical character in racist minstrel shows popular in the period.

1883 The U.S. Supreme Court declares the Civil Rights Act of 1875 unconstitutional. The act had deemed discrimination in many public places illegal.

1909 The National Association for the Advancement of Colored People (NAACP) is founded.

1920 The Nineteenth Amendment to the Constitution gives women the right to vote.

1954 In *Brown v. Board of Education of Topeka*, the U.S. Supreme Court rules unanimously that segregation in public schools is unconstitutional.

1954 November 14: Condoleezza Rice is born in Birmingham, Alabama.

1955 In Montgomery, Alabama, Rosa Parks is arrested for refusing to give her seat to a white man and move to the back of the bus, where black people were forced to sit. The yearlong boycott of the city's buses (led by Martin Luther King Jr.) ends when the U.S. Supreme Court declares Montgomery's segregated transportation system unconstitutional.

1957 Fred Shuttlesworth, Charles K. Steele, Martin Luther King Jr., and many other civil rights leaders establish the Southern Christian Leadership Conference (SCLC) to end segregation through nonviolent protest and civil disobedience.

1957 President Dwight D. Eisenhower sends federal troops to Little Rock, Arkansas, to protect black students after the state militia prevents them from entering a public high school. The governor is forced to comply with U.S. desegregation laws.

1960 John F. Kennedy is elected the thirty-fifth president of the United States.

1962 Birmingham Commissioner of Public Safety Theophilus Eugene "Bull" Connor closes public recreational facilities to avoid integration.

1962 John Glenn becomes the first American astronaut to orbit the earth.

1963 April 16: Martin Luther King Jr. is jailed during civil rights protests in Birmingham. During his imprisonment, he writes his famous "Letter from Birmingham Jail," urging eight fellow clergymen to support the cause of desegregation.

1963 May 2: Hundreds of students participate in the Children's Crusade for civil rights in Birmingham.

1963 August 28: A crowd of 250,000 attends the March on Washington, D.C. Martin Luther King Jr. delivers his "I Have a Dream" speech from the steps of the Lincoln Memorial.

1963 September 15: Four young girls are killed and more than twenty people are injured when the predominantly black Sixteenth Street Baptist Church in Birmingham is bombed. In the aftermath of protests later that day, sixteen-year-old Johnny Robinson is shot in the back by police, and thirteen-year-old Virgil Wade is shot by a group of teenagers while riding his bike. Both teenagers are black.

1963   November 22: President John F. Kennedy is assassinated in Dallas, Texas.

1963   November 22: Lyndon B. Johnson is sworn in as the thirty-sixth president of the United States.

1964   July 2: President Johnson signs the Civil Rights Act of 1964, which forbids discrimination based on race, color, religion, or national origin.

1965   Congress passes the Voting Rights Act; states can no longer restrict voter eligibility by requiring literacy tests or poll taxes, and federal oversight of elections is broadened.

1966   The Rice family moves to Tuscaloosa, Alabama.

1968   April 4: Martin Luther King Jr. is assassinated in Memphis. Riots break out in cities across the country.

1968   June 5: Robert "Bobby" Kennedy is assassinated in Los Angeles.

1968   August 20: Soviet forces invade Czechoslovakia.

1968   August 26–29: At the Democratic Convention in

Chicago, protests against U.S. involvement in the Vietnam War turn bloody when crowds clash with police.

1968 The Rice family moves to Denver.

1974 August 9: Richard Nixon resigns as thirty-seventh president of the United States after attempting to cover up his role in break-ins at the Democratic Party headquarters in Washington, D.C.'s Watergate complex.

1974 Condoleezza Rice begins graduate school at the University of Notre Dame.

1976 James Earl "Jimmy" Carter is elected the thirty-ninth president of the United States.

1980 The United States and approximately sixty other countries boycott the Summer Olympics in Moscow in response to the Soviet invasion of Afghanistan.

1981 Condoleezza Rice receives her PhD from the Graduate School of International Studies at the University of Denver and joins the faculty at Stanford University in California.

1985 Mikhail Gorbachev becomes general secretary of the Communist Party of the Soviet Union.

1985 Angelena Rice dies in Denver.

1988 George H. W. Bush, who was vice president under President Ronald Reagan, is elected the forty-first president of the United States.

1989–1991 Condoleezza Rice serves on the National Security Council under President George H. W. Bush.

1989 November 9: The Berlin Wall is opened.

1991 Boris Yeltsin seizes power from Mikhail Gorbachev, and the USSR is disbanded.

1993 Condoleezza Rice becomes provost of Stanford University.

2000 George W. Bush is elected the forty-third president of the United States.

2000 John Rice dies in Palo Alto, California.

2001 January 20: Condoleezza Rice is appointed national security advisor.

2005 January 26: Condoleezza Rice is appointed secretary of state.

glossary

Abernathy, Ralph (1926–1990): Civil rights leader, a founder of the Southern Christian Leadership Conference (SCLC), and the man Martin Luther King Jr. described as his best friend. In 1968, when King was shot, Abernathy held him in his arms as he died. Weeks later, Abernathy went on to lead the Poor People's Campaign march on Washington. He continued to spearhead efforts to improve the lives of disenfranchised Americans of all races until his death.

Affirmative Action: Policy of offering increased economic, political, and social opportunities to minorities, women, and other underrepresented groups with the goal of increasing diversity and correcting years of discrimination. The practice is the subject of much controversy.

Albright, Tenley (1935–): American figure skater, winner of the silver medal at the 1952 Olympics and the gold medal at the 1956 Olympics. Albright took up skating when she was a girl as part of her recovery from polio. In 1961, she graduated from Harvard University and became a surgeon.

Attica Correctional Facility: In September 1971, inmates of this New York prison revolted to protest bad conditions, taking control of the facility and holding a number of guards hostage. The riot ended after four days with ten prison employees and twenty-nine prisoners dead.

Bach, Johann Sebastian (1685–1750): German composer highly regarded for his religious pieces and organ works.

Beethoven, Ludwig van (1770–1827): Influential pianist and composer of symphonies. Before he turned thirty, he began to lose his hearing, but he continued to produce extraordinary pieces despite his deafness later in life.

Berlin Wall (1961–1989): Guarded barrier separating West Berlin from East Berlin and East Germany during the Cold War. By the early 1950s, Germany and its capital city, Berlin, had been divided into two territories: West Germany, allied with the United States, Great Britain and France, and East Germany, allied with the Soviet Union. The Wall became symbolic of the divide between communist Eastern Europe and the democratic West. The Berlin Wall collapsed on

November 9, 1989, ushering in a series of events that unified East and West Germany and ended the Cold War.

Black Panthers: Activists in Oakland, California, founded the Black Panther Party for Self-defense to protect their communities from police brutality. The influential party grew controversial when it began to call for radical measures such as arming all blacks. Conflicts between the Black Panthers and the police were common in the late 1960s and early 1970s.

Bond, Julian (1940–): Black activist and civil rights leader who helped found the Student Nonviolent Coordinating Committee (SNCC) and was elected to the Georgia state legislature as a representative and then as a senator. For many years Bond was the president of the Southern Poverty Law Center and the national chairman of the NAACP.

Brezhnev, Leonid (1906–1982): Communist leader of the Soviet Union from 1964 to 1982.

Brown, Jim (1936–): Running back for the Cleveland Browns football team for nine years.

Bush, George H. W. (1924–): Elected the forty-first president of the United States. Joined the U.S. Navy at age eighteen, becoming its youngest flier, and served in World War II, earning the Distinguished Flying Cross for bravery in action, among other awards. Later Bush attended Yale

University, then moved to Texas, where he started an oil business and became active in politics. After serving as vice president under Ronald Reagan (1981–1989), Bush served as president from 1989 to 1993. Nine months into his presidency, the Berlin Wall was torn down. When Iraq invaded neighboring Kuwait, Bush sent U.S. troops to join allied forces in expelling Saddam Hussein's forces from its neighbor during the 1991 Persian Gulf War.

Bush, George W. (1946–): One of four sons of George H. W. Bush. He spent six years as governor of Texas before being elected the forty-third president of the United States (2001–2009). Within eight months of his taking office, on September 11, 2001, terrorists flew two commercial airplanes into the World Trade Center towers in New York and one into the Pentagon in Washington; a fourth hijacked plane crashed in a field in Pennsylvania. In all, nearly three thousand people died. President Bush declared a war on terror and launched military campaigns in Afghanistan in 2001 and Iraq in 2003.

Carmichael, Stokely (1941–1998): Black activist, a founder of the SNCC, and the originator of the motto "Black Power." Carmichael was a good friend of the Rice family and frequently lectured in John W. Rice's courses at Denver University.

Carter, James Earl "Jimmy" (1924–): Thirty-ninth president of the United States (1977–1981). After his bid for reelection failed, he founded the Carter Center, which works to advance global peace and human rights. Carter is also an ardent supporter of Habitat for Humanity, an organization through which volunteers build houses for those in need. He remains active in international diplomacy and was awarded the Nobel Peace Prize in 2002.

Civil Rights Act of 1964: Historic legislation passed during the civil rights movement and signed by President Lyndon B. Johnson that prohibited segregation in places of public accommodation.

Clinton, William Jefferson "Bill" (1946–): Forty-second president of the United States (1993–2001). Clinton served during a time of relative peace and economic expansion. In 1998, Congress began impeachment proceedings against him after he was accused of misconduct with a White House intern; he apologized to the nation, and his approval rating remained high until he left office. Clinton's wife, Hillary Rodham Clinton, was elected to the U.S. Senate and became secretary of state under President Barack Obama.

Cold War (c. 1947–1991): State of political hostility and military threats that existed after World War II between the United States and the Soviet Union.

Communism: Political ideology in which the central government controls the economy. In contrast to democracies, leaders in communist governments rise from within a single political party, and the state places strict limits on personal freedoms and political expression.

Connor, Theophilus Eugene "Bull" (1887–1973): Public safety commissioner of Birmingham, Alabama, during the 1960s and a staunch supporter of segregation known for his brutality.

Cuban Missile Crisis: In October 1962, the United States discovered that the Soviet Union was installing nuclear missile sites in Cuba, ninety miles off the coast of Florida. President Kennedy demanded that the missiles be removed and instituted a naval blockade of the island. After tense negotiations and close confrontations that many believed would lead to nuclear war, the USSR acceded, with concessions on both sides.

Dickens, Charles (1812–1870): Famous English novelist whose works include *A Tale of Two Cities*, *David Copperfield*, *Bleak House*, and *A Christmas Carol*.

Farrakhan, Louis (1933–): Black activist, social critic, and leader of the Nation of Islam, an organization that champions black nationalism and cultural awareness through the teachings of Islam.

German unification (1989–1991): Diplomatic process at the beginning of the 1990s that united West Germany and East Germany. After the fall of the Berlin Wall in November 1989, leaders negotiated a settlement unifying the two countries into a single German state.

Gorbachev, Mikhail (1931–): General Secretary of the Communist Party of the Soviet Union (1985–1991), then elected president of Russia (1990–1991). Gorbachev presided during a time of momentous changes, most notably the formation of an elected parliament in the USSR, the re-unification of Germany, and the end of the Cold War. His liberalizing policies made him popular in the West, where he often was referred to as Gorby.

Gregory, Dick (1932–): Came to fame as an edgy comedian who confronted racial prejudice. Over the years, he has developed into a writer, social critic, and health activist.

Hamer, Fannie Lou (1917–1977): The granddaughter of slaves, Hamer became an activist when she was forced to leave the plantation where she was a sharecropper after trying to register to vote. In 1964, she led an alternate delegation to the Democratic National Convention to challenge the all-white Mississippi delegation.

Hesburgh, Theodore (1917–): Roman Catholic priest and president of the University of Notre Dame (1952–1987). During his term of office, Notre Dame became a coeducational school.

Historically Black Colleges and Universities (HBCU): Institutions founded specifically for the education of black people. The first all-black colleges include Grambling State University (founded in 1901), Howard University (1867), Meharry Medical College (1876), Miles College (1898),

Morehouse College (1867), Spelman College (1881), Stillman College (1876), Tuskegee University (1880), and Wilberforce University (1856).

Hoover Institution on War, Revolution and Peace: Organization on the Stanford campus that produces research on domestic and international affairs.

Johnson, Frank (1918–1999): Federal judge whose rulings helped end segregation in the South. Johnson received so many death threats that his family was under federal protection for more than twenty years.

Johnson, Lyndon Baines (1908–1973): When President Kennedy was assassinated in Dallas in November 1963, Vice President Johnson was sworn in and became the thirty-sixth president of the United States. The following year, he was elected to the office, and he served from 1963 to 1969. He signed into law the Civil Rights Act of 1964 and the Voting Rights Act of 1965. He also escalated American involvement in the Vietnam War.

Joint Chiefs of Staff: Group of military officials who advise the president and nonmilitary leaders of the Defense Department. The Joint Chiefs is made up of the leaders of the four branches of the military—the U.S. Army, Navy, Air Force, and Marines—and the chairman, who is generally considered the president's top military advisor.

glossary

Kennedy, John Fitzgerald (1917–1963): Thirty-fifth president of the United States (and first Catholic to be elected). Kennedy ran on a platform of commitment to civil rights legislation, and it became a priority of his presidency. He also established the Peace Corps, which trains Americans who volunteer to live and work in developing countries. Kennedy was assassinated in Dallas on November 22, 1963.

Kennedy, Robert Francis "Bobby" (1925–1968): Appointed U.S. attorney general by President Kennedy, his older brother, he remained in that position under President Johnson until he left in 1964 to run successfully for the U.S. Senate from New York. In 1968, while running in the Democratic primary for president, he was assassinated in Los Angeles.

Khrushchev, Nikita (1894–1971): First secretary of the Communist Party of the Soviet Union from 1953 to 1964 and premier from 1958 to 1964. After the death of dictator Josef Stalin, who ordered political purges and mass murders during his twenty-five-year reign, Khrushchev declared a desire for "peaceful coexistence" with Western governments. In practice, however, he often pursued a more confrontational stance with the United States and its allies. In 1964, he was replaced by Leonid Brezhnev.

King, Jr., Martin Luther (1929–1968): Baptist minister, civil rights activist, and advocate of nonviolent civil disobedience. In 1955 and 1956, King led the Montgomery bus boycott, an early demonstration of the power of peaceful resistance, and in 1957, he helped found the Southern Christian Leadership Conference (SCLC). His powerful speeches, including the "I Have a Dream" speech on the steps of the Lincoln Memorial, influenced the nation and helped lead to the passage of the Civil Rights Act of 1964; he was awarded the Nobel Peace Prize that year. King was assassinated in Memphis in 1968.

Korbel, Josef (1909–1977): Czech diplomat, founder of Denver University's Graduate School of International Studies, specialist on the Soviet Union, and father of former secretary of state Madeleine Albright. Professor Korbel was an influential mentor for Condoleezza Rice and inspired her to pursue a PhD in international politics.

Kosygin, Alexei (1904–1980): Premier of the Soviet Union from 1964 to 1980. Initially, Kosygin shared power with Leonid Brezhnev and Nikolai Podgorny (chairman of the Presidium), but gradually Brezhnev assumed control and Kosygin retired.

Ku Klux Klan (KKK): White supremacist organization founded in Tennessee in 1866 by Confederate soldiers returning from the Civil War; they opposed Reconstruction and civil rights for blacks. Men dressed in white sheets and hoods to frighten their victims, whom they pursued in nighttime raids; they often maimed or killed blacks and Northern sympathizers. The Klan died down during the 1880s, only to rise again at the turn of the century and spread across the country. At its peak during the 1920s, membership was estimated at four million. Today the KKK is officially listed as a terrorist organization by the U.S. government.

***The Mickey Mouse Club* (1955–1959):** Walt Disney TV program featuring mouse ear–wearing "Mouseketeers," talented preteens and teenagers who sang, acted, and danced.

Mozart, Wolfgang Amadeus (1756–1791): Prolific Austrian composer of more than six hundred works, including symphonies, operas, and piano music. A musical prodigy, he began playing as a child before princes and monarchs throughout Europe.

National Security Council: Group of foreign policy experts and specialists who advise the president on national security and foreign affairs. Led by the national security advisor, the National Security Council helps coordinate the efforts of various departments and agencies involved in shaping the nation's foreign policy.

Netanyahu, Benjamin "Bibi" (1949–): Born in Israel, attended high school in the United States, then returned to Israel from 1967 to 1972 for mandatory military service. Netanyahu was prime minister from 1996 to 1999 and assumed the office again in 2009.

Nixon, Richard Milhous (1913–1994): Thirty-seventh president of the United States (1969–1974); also served in the House of Representatives and as a senator from California. Nixon was vice president under President Dwight Eisenhower from 1953 to 1961. As president, Nixon negotiated a cease-fire with North Vietnam in 1973, ending U.S. involvement in the Vietnam War. In 1974, he resigned to avoid impeachment after the Watergate scandal erupted.

Parks, Rosa (1913–2005): On December 1, 1955, in Montgomery, Alabama, Rosa Parks refused to give her seat to a white man and move to the back of a city bus. She was arrested for her defiance of the Jim Crow laws enforcing segregation. In protest, Martin Luther King Jr. led the 381-day boycott that ended in desegregation of the buses.

Persian Gulf War (1991): A conflict in the Middle East between Iraq and international forces led by the United States. After Iraqi dictator Saddam Hussein's forces invaded neighboring Kuwait in August 1990, U.S. President George H. W. Bush assembled an international coalition of forces that successfully expelled Hussein's forces from Kuwait and pushed them back to the Iraqi capital.

Powell, Colin (1937–): Four-star general in the U.S. Army and chairman of the Joint Chiefs of Staff (1989–1993) during the Persian Gulf War. President George W. Bush appointed Powell secretary of state (2001–2005), making Powell the first African American to hold that office.

Prokofiev, Sergei (1891–1953): Twentieth-century Russian composer.

Provost: Chief academic officer of a college or university; second-in-command to the university president. Responsible for managing academic resources and the university budget.

Putin, Vladimir (1952–): President of Russia from 1999 to 2008; former member of the Soviet secret police organization known as the KGB (Committee for State Security). Although term limits prevented Putin from running for the office again, he was confirmed as prime minister in 2008 under the new Russian president, Dmitri Medvedev.

Reagan, Ronald (1911–2004): Ronald Reagan was a popular movie actor, TV star, and governor of California before he was elected the fortieth president of the United States (1981–1989). His economic policies reduced government regulation of business and cut taxes; he also cut spending on many social welfare programs and increased military spending. His administration had a tense relationship with the Soviet Union, which he called an evil empire, and his anti-Soviet rhetoric, combined with the U.S. military buildup, escalated the arms race. Gradually, President Reagan began to see Gorbachev as a true reformer and pursued more conciliatory relations with the Soviet leader.

Scowcroft, Brent (1925–): U.S. Air Force lieutenant general who served twice as national security advisor: from 1974 to 1977, under President Gerald Ford, and from 1989 to 1993, under President George H. W. Bush.

Sharecropping: System by which people work on a farm they don't own in return for a share of the money from the sale of crops. Generally, sharecroppers make little or no money for their efforts.

Shockley, William (1910–1989): Scientist who shared the 1956 Nobel Prize for Physics for coinventing the transistor. Later in his career, he promoted a number of controversial theories about differences between races; he believed that blacks were genetically inferior to whites.

Shostakovich, Dimitri (1906–1975): Twentieth-century Russian composer.

Shuttlesworth, Fred (1922–): Baptist minister, civil rights activist, and a founder, along with Martin Luther King Jr., of the Southern Christian Leadership Conference.

Smith, Tommie, and Carlos, John: American track stars. At the 1968 Summer Olympics, Tommie Smith won the gold medal in the 200-meter race and John Carlos won the bronze. During the awards ceremony, they raised their arms in a black power salute. An uproar followed, and the International Olympic Committee suspended Smith and Carlos from the U.S. team.

Southern Christian Leadership Conference (SCLC):
Formed in 1957 by Fred Shuttlesworth, Ralph Abernathy,
and Martin Luther King Jr., among others, with King as its
first president. The goal of the organization was to actively
pursue racial equality through nonviolent means.

Stanford University: Institution of higher education based
in Silicon Valley in Northern California. Founded in 1891
by former California governor and senator Leland
Stanford and his wife, Jane Lathrop Stanford, the university
counted women, an African American, and future U.S.
president Herbert Hoover among the students in its first
graduating class.

Student Nonviolent Coordinating Committee (SNCC):
Political organization that advocated nonviolent protest
against racial injustice through such activities as sit-ins.
The SNCC played a major role in organizing the Freedom
Riders, interracial activists who took bus trips through the
segregated South.

Tet Offensive (1968): On January 31, 1968, in violation of
a truce called for the lunar new year, or Tet, North Vietnam
launched a major attack on several South Vietnamese cities.
Media coverage of the attacks increased U.S. opposition to
the Vietnam War.

Union of Soviet Socialist Republics (USSR): Also known
as the Soviet Union. At one time the largest country in the
world, comprising fifteen political divisions called republics.

Until 1991, when the USSR dissolved, the republics had little autonomy. The Communist Party controlled the central government, which was based in Moscow.

United Nations: International organization founded in 1945 to provide a world forum for all nations to promote peace and security, defend human rights, and alleviate disease and poverty.

Verdi, Giuseppe (1813–1901): Italian composer who wrote popular operas such as *Aïda* and *La Traviata*. He is well known for his "Triumphal March."

Vietnam War (1964–1973): Conflict in Southeast Asia during the Cold War in which the United States fought on behalf of the South Vietnamese government against the Northern Viet Cong and its communist allies. As President Lyndon Johnson escalated America's military involvement in the region, the war became deeply unpopular at home and sparked nationwide protests. President Richard Nixon withdrew all remaining U.S. troops from Vietnam in 1973; the war ended in 1975 after the fall of Saigon, the Vietnamese capital, and the victory of the North Vietnamese communist forces.

Voting Rights Act of 1965: Landmark civil rights legislation that prohibited literacy tests and poll taxes, which had been used in the Jim Crow South to prevent blacks from voting.

Wallace, George (1919–1998): Four-term governor of Alabama, unsuccessful candidate for the U.S. presidency, and outspoken segregationist during the 1950s and 1960s. In the late 1970s, Wallace became religious and changed his views, apologizing to African Americans for his behavior.

Watergate scandal: In the summer of 1972, five men broke into the Democratic National Committee headquarters in the Watergate complex in Washington, D.C. The men were arrested on charges of burglary and were eventually linked to the reelection campaign of President Richard Nixon. The subsequent effort to cover up these events led to the highest levels of the U.S. government. Eventually, President Nixon was implicated in the cover-up and resigned to avoid impeachment.

X, Malcolm (1925–1965): Born Malcolm Little, he educated himself while in prison for robbery, where he changed his last name to X because it was not a "slave name," a name given to his ancestors by white slaveholders. He became a leader of the Nation of Islam, gaining fame for speeches urging blacks to defend their rights "by any means necessary." He left the organization after repeated conflicts with its leadership but did not moderate his outspoken views. Malcolm X was assassinated in 1965; three members of the Nation of Islam were convicted of his murder.